Ken Sales

WHITEWATER DEVILS

Jack Boudreau

Jack Boudreau

WHITE
WATER
DEVILS

Adventure on Wild Waters

JACK BOUDREAU

CAITLIN PRESS
HALFMOON BAY · BRITISH COLUMBIA

Caitlin Press Inc.
8100 Alderwood Road,
Halfmoon Bay, BC V0N 1Y1
www.caitlin-press.com

Text design by Rachel Page
Cover design by the house
Printed in Canada

Uncredited photos are from the author's collection.
Cover images: Top photo by Ian Norn; bottom image courtesy Bill Blackburn.

Caitlin Press Inc. acknowledges financial support from the Government of Canada through the Canada Book Fund and the Canada Council for the Arts, and from the Province of British Columbia through the British Columbia Arts Council and the Book Publisher's Tax Credit.

 Canada Council for the Arts   Conseil des Arts du Canada    BRITISH COLUMBIA ARTS COUNCIL

Library and Archives Canada Cataloguing in Publication

Boudreau, Jack, 1933-
    Whitewater devils : adventure on wild waters / Jack Boudreau.

ISBN 978-1-894759-46-5

    1. Canoes and canoeing—British Columbia—History. 2. British Columbia—Description and travel—1951-1980. 3. Rivers—British Columbia—Anecdotes. 4. Lakes—British Columbia—Anecdotes. 5. Voyageurs. 6. Expo 67 (Montréal, Québec). I. Title.

GV776.15.B7B69 2010   797.12209711   C2010-905737-6

This book is dedicated to the pioneers who travelled our waterways in flimsy crafts, canoes and rafts that were often little more than death traps. The number of people lost throughout the years cannot be measured as often no records were kept of their travels. Besides, many people deliberately avoided others and kept their business to themselves.

Records that were kept tell of people so traumatized with fear during trips along our rivers that they refused to get into a boat or canoe for the rest of their lives. My mother used to tell us of an incident where the people in a narrow riverboat all panicked and crowded to the same side of the boat. Only the presence of mind of two people prevented a tragedy; and a tragedy it would have been because there were no life jackets available and most could not swim.

I also want to pay tribute to the respect often shown to women in the past. For instance, whenever a woman came into our home my father would stand up. Even if he was eating, he would rise and acknowledge her presence. Many years have passed since I have noticed anyone doing this sort of thing. Chivalry may not be dead, but it certainly has been mortally wounded.

—Jack Boudreau

CONTENTS

INTRODUCTION

It has always been my desire to write a book about the transformation in water transport during the last century in British Columbia. During my years with the Ministry of Forests I had more opportunities than most people to observe many of our stunning rivers with their canyons, rapids and whirlpools. A century ago people travelled our waterways on rafts, scows and crude dugout canoes. There were no life preservers and many of the pioneer people could not swim; the end result was staggering losses to drowning. Now, some of the wildest rivers have been tamed by people in jet boats, huge rafts and kayaks. One cannot help but wonder what the next century will bring. Perhaps walking on water in some form or other will be an everyday occurrence.

But for these modern-day adventurers, there is another world, remote from our highways, that holds one captive with its stunning beauty and silent timelessness. Unfortunately, this is a world many people never encounter.

One of the greatest experiences of my life occurred on a forest fire during the summer of 1985. We had a rash of lightning strikes along the Torpy and McGregor watersheds and out of them arose several fires, one of considerable size in the East Torpy Valley. Because the forests were dry, the helicopter companies had their choppers on minimum hours, which meant that they got paid a given number of hours flying time per day regardless of how little they were used. Since we were just using the choppers to fly crews in and out of the valley to attack the fire, they were used only for a maximum of half that amount of pay. I discussed this with my superior and suggested that this was the opportunity of a lifetime for me. The other forest officer on the fire offered to cover for me, and since we had a second chopper on site, we were covered in case of an emergency medivac. I agreed that I would turn in no time card while engaged in this adventure, and because I signed the flight slips I knew how much the helicopter companies were paid. Hence, there was no extra cost whatever to the Ministry of Forests.

What a memorable day that turned out to be. Pilot Blair Wood and I covered an enormous area of the Rocky Mountains around and east of Mt. Alexander. In fact, we flew the tanks right out of fuel.

Many species of wildlife were viewed that day, including mountain goats only a few rotor lengths away from us. If ever I were to win a lottery, I could not think of a better way to spend it than to replicate that day. We saw beautiful alpine lakes surrounded by wildflowers, and cliffs that towered straight into the heavens as if God had chopped them off with a giant machete. In one spot we flew right inside a gigantic break in a mountain where a raging stream poured out of a confined glacier. As we hovered about 100 metres (330 feet) above the stream I looked up to see the sheer cliffs on either side of us almost closed tight and the rock walls coming straight down on either side of the stream. In other words, we were hovering stationary in a place one could only get to with a helicopter. There was no other possible way of viewing what was one of the most impressive sights I have ever seen.

But things have changed and now it may be possible for that canyon to be accessed by people such as Brent Gobbi and Kevin Fitzsimmons. In their state-of-the-art jet boats, these men have ventured along rivers, over logs and downed trees, and through rapids that I always considered impassable. In fact, even after watching them I still find it hard to believe the rugged water they travel through.

As to the glorious sights Blair and I viewed that day, it is a description that fits many areas of our majestic province, and few people get to know it as well as these adventurers and our wilderness guides. In this book I describe the life of a guide with 54 years of experience in the Quesnel area of BC. Betty Frank is her name and outdoor living was her game. Who says that guiding is men's work?

Whitewater Devils is a collection of adventures on wild water from raging rivers to mighty lakes with 5.5-metre (18-foot) waves and fog so thick that visibility is limited to the length of a canoe. It is also a collection of stories about people kayaking over falls and through canyons where angels should fear to tread.

A shining example of an endurance canoe trip was the one to Expo '67 in Montreal in celebration of Canada's 100th birthday. One hundred gallant men called Les Voyageurs left Rocky Mountain House, Alberta, in ten 8-metre (26-foot) canoes. Representing eight provinces and two territories, they travelled 5,282 kilometres (3,283 miles), the trip taking them across such major lakes as Winnipeg, Lake of the Woods, Superior, Nipissing, Huron and its northern portion called Georgian Bay. They also traversed at least 68 portages, some as much as 30 kilometres (19 miles) in length. After 104 days of travel, the Manitoba team paddled into the Expo site as the winners, with each Voyageur claiming the first prize of $2,500. BC came in a proud second with $2,000 per person, and Alberta took third with $1,500 each.

There is an abundance of canoeing adventures such as the "Canoe across Canada" effort of Geoff and Pamela MacDonald of Calgary, Alberta. Their trip from Victoria, BC, to the Saskatchewan/Manitoba border was filled with adventure and gruelling portages. I am extremely grateful to them for allowing me to tell their story.

Ian Norn of Prince George shows and explains how the art of kayaking has taken him to roaring rapids and canyons that were out of the reach of humans a few short years ago. He is involved in a sport where people kayak over falls and through canyons that still appear impassable to me. A glimpse of Ian and friends at play can be viewed at www.paddlepg.ca.

Other adventures cover such things as wildlife photography, namely Leon Lorenz and his close-up work with animals, especially grizzly bears. Leon's work speaks for itself and his lack of fear around bears surprises me. In one case a mama grizzly with a cub carries a dead salmon up the riverbank a scant few metres distant from him. Leon backs his stories up with photographic proof, and his finished product is second to none.

No sooner had I agreed to do a story on his adventures than I got word from him that he had been charged by two grizzlies and had come within a whisper of getting mauled or killed. The scary scene was captured on HD video and was shown on the nightly news for several weeks. Truthfully, Leon ranks among the coolest-headed woodsmen ever to come to my attention.

This story is told in the following pages along with many other exciting tales. So grab a coffee, sit back and enjoy these adventures by people who live for excitement and will accept nothing less.

—Jack Boudreau

I.

Beneath the Waters

There are people in this world who find excitement in doing what to others appears to be madness. For instance, how many of us are prepared to don a couple of air tanks and go beneath ice into a world of total darkness? I have never felt the desire to do such a thing; just the thought of slipping into scuba gear and going down 50 metres (165 feet) under the ice or crawling through a pipe beneath a river gives me a vibrant surge of claustrophobia.

For Prince George resident Russ Logan, scuba diving started out as a form of entertainment. He was practising diving at Bear Lake north of Prince George back in 1960 when the police approached him and asked for his assistance in what they described as a suspected drowning of a young girl. Her body was found shortly after in 3 metres (10 feet) of water.

Practising diving in Cluculz Lake.

That was the start of what turned out to be a career in diving and eventually training divers, including members of the police who had received initial training from the force. From that humble beginning, Russ soon found his talent was required at many locations, such as in the Arctic Ocean near Tuktoyaktuk, or Tuk as it is commonly known. All the supplies carried on an Imperial Oil barge were swept off and dumped into 10 metres (33 feet) of water. When I questioned Russ about the difficulty in recovering the supplies he informed me that it was rather simple because he was working in crystal clear water. That was not always the case; more often than not he worked in complete darkness where everything was done by touch.

An example of what Russ had to contend with was described in the *Prince George Citizen:*

> If Russ Logan suffers from a twinge of claustrophobia now and again, no one can really blame him. Like today for instance. Russ, a part-time professional diver, has spent several hours in the Nechako River this week coupling intake pipes of a new city pump house installation. Today his job sent him swimming through 85 feet of 36 inch pipe beneath four feet of the riverbed. Not a job for someone needing the freedom of the wide open spaces, he admits.
>
> But for the young diver such situations are encountered every time he enters the cold, muddy waters of the Nechako—and many other northern rivers and lakes every winter. "You can't see anything when you're down there," he says, explaining that all the work he undertakes is done by feel. To the non-diver the prospect of jumping into the near-freezing waters of the Nechako River is an unsettling thought.
>
> To Logan, an expert diver with many hours of deep water work under his belt—including many a session below the ice—the undertaking is seen as "another day, another dollar."
>
> Although equipped for maximum warmth, the cold still penetrates his rubber-like diving suit, yet he

manages to work for prolonged periods of time in the water. Tuesday he spent seven hours within the dammed-up area where the work is going on. Russ' job involves bolting together sections of pipe lowered into a trench dug into the riverbed. When the project is completed it will increase water intake to the pump-house's maximum of four million gallons per day, although that amount of water is not always necessary.

I wrote about another example of Russ's expertise in my previous book, *Trappers & Trailblazers*. Four men were trapped in trees in Williston Lake during the summer of 1969. After the men were rescued, Russ and a co-diver went to the location to salvage their boat and supplies from over 14 metres (45 feet) of water.

There was a constant danger of getting tangled in the huge amount of debris in the water, such as in Williston Lake. This inspired a diver named Kerry Gibbons to develop a case to cover the lines and tanks of the scuba gear and prevent entrapment and certain death. Along with the cover, a helmet with a built-in light was used for working in the darkness prevalent in deep water. This light was not always a help; down in murky water, such as that in the Fraser River, almost everything has to be done by touch.

Russ displays the improved, covered scuba gear.

A challenge worth remembering occurred when a Grumman Widgeon twin-engine plane owned by Ben Ginter crashed into McConnell Lake 480 kilometres (290 miles) northwest of Prince George. The pilot, Stuart Lockart, had been transporting two prospectors employed by Ginter. They all survived the

Ben Ginter's airplane coming up out of McConnell Lake.

crash and swam to shore using sleeping bags as floatation devices, then watched as the plane sank to the murky lake bottom into 50 metres (165 feet) of water. Ideally, the divers should have had helium to use at that depth, but none was available.

Russ and assistant diver John Chato found the plane by working off a raft that had been constructed just for that purpose. The two divers had a rough time working in the extreme cold and pressure but finally managed to find the aircraft. When questioned about the depth of the dive, Russ explained that they figured out the amount of time they could spend down at the plane before they left the surface, stressing the point that it is best to do the calculations when one's mind is clear.

But perseverance prevailed, and as the raft had a winch on board, the plane was being lifted and dragged toward shore when another problem arose. The winch jumped a cog and the line broke, allowing the plane to head back down into the water. And then, just as it would have in the air, the plane glided underwater for over half kilometre before it settled on the bottom again in much shallower water. Luckily, Russ had attached

Ben Ginter's airplane after it was repaired.

The crew at McConnell Lake. Russ on the left and Denny McCartney second from right.

a poly rope to the plane. The rope floated and this made the plane easy to find again. The next attempt at removing the plane was successful. Once the crew got the plane to shore, a man named Denny McCartney made it operational again and flew it out to be put back in service.

An interesting footnote to this story was that the boat used in the retrieval of the plane was a float off a Junkers F13 aircraft owed by Prince George Airways and named *The City of Prince George*. This plane had crashed just off the lake during August 1966.

Old-timers may recall that this same plane was involved in the search for two prospectors, Emil Kading and Robert Martin, who along with their pilot were lost in the Pelly Mountains in the Far North for almost two months. The year was 1930 when the pilot, Paddy Burke, crashed near the Pelly Mountains. The pilot died but the other two men were finally rescued just before Christmas by famed Yukon pilot Everett Wasson and his guide, Joe Walsh.

Being a diver is one thing, but being a diver's wife is surely another. Russ's wife Roni explained what it was like to wait at home when she knew he was on a difficult dive. She described the terror she felt when two RCMP officers came to her place of work and asked if they could speak with her outside. Russ was away on a dive at that time so we can appreciate the thoughts that ran through her mind. Thankfully it turned out to be totally unrelated to Russ and so a great wave of relief swept over her. Roni also told about the many trips they made abroad; often diving was included somewhere along the trail.

Russ must have had something going for him because a group of doctors and businessmen got together and paid his way through university as well as his diving training costs. Although Russ spent several years working for CKPG and the *Prince George Citizen,* it seems apparent to me that he found his niche in life when he got into diving.

But diving is not a way of life suited to everyone. Imagine crawling through 25 metres (83 feet) of pipe beneath a river; certainly no claustrophobic person is going in there. One of Russ's jobs entailed putting sections of pipe together at the bottom of a river. As he worked away, he felt more than usual pressure and realized that the bank of the trench had slid and trapped his legs. He tugged on the life-support rope that led to the surface but there was no response from above. With no other option, Russ dug with his hands until he managed to free himself. When he rose to the surface he found that his assistant was not on duty; he had decided to take a coffee break and left his post unattended. A bit of overdue justice

Dan Hayes going into the pipe beneath the Nechako River.

came down the pipe when Russ fired the fellow into the water with the suggestion that he see how long he could hold his breath.

The unexpected was often the norm when diving into darkness, such as the time Russ went down to clean out the trash rack for a local pulp mill. A search turned up a drowned moose that had got caught in the mechanism. A rope was tied to the animal and it was towed clear, allowing normal operations once again.

The dangers involved in diving to great depths have been recognized for many years. There is a strange effect known as "rapture of the deep" that can overcome a diver. In some cases people have continued diving to ever greater depths without the realization that they are in trouble. Such may have been the case with Ann Gunderson of Prince George when she went missing on a diving trip. She was diving off Andres Island in the Bahamas with co-diver Archie Forfar, where they were attempting to beat the old diving record, using normal air, of 132 metres (437 feet) set by two Americans in 1968. It was suspected that they passed the 144-metre (475-foot) level when they disappeared. Ross Ellis of West Palm Beach was another diver at the scene; he stated that the attempt ended in tragedy despite assistance from five support divers and special equipment designed by Forfar to buoy them to the surface in an emergency. One explanation presented was that they had experienced the so-called rapture of the deep. It was also noted that dives below 45 metres (150 feet) should not be attempted by sport divers. Nitrogen should be removed and helium added at a ratio available on charts.

A common myth states that a diver uses oxygen in the air tanks while diving. In fact, this cannot be, as oxygen becomes poisonous below 10 metres (33 feet). It is known as oxygen toxicity.

Generally speaking, the bends can be prevented by constantly exhaling as one heads toward the surface. The object is to remove as much air as possible from the lungs in direct proportion to the loss of pressure; the lungs keep expanding and this air must be expelled to relieve the pressure.

The date was May 29, 1970. The temperature was -7°C (20°F). The employer was Canadian National Telecommunications. The mission was a trip by air to Great Beaver Lake to retrieve a Bombardier Nodwell snow packer from 7 metres (23 feet) of water. The machine was being used to pack a trail for cross-country snowmobile racing when it plunged through the ice. Russ accomplished the mission by digging in the mud and muskeg until he found the hook in the drawbar and attached a line to it. The other end of the line held a buoy, which floated just below ice level. This made the buoy easy to locate after the ice went off the lake. The insurance company sold the retrieved snow machine to the highest bidder, which was Purden Ski Village.

Another adventurous day started when Russ and fellow diver Dick Wood were called to Williston Lake because a tugboat had sunk. While it may seem impossible for a tugboat to sink, I have it from several individuals that 5- to 10-metre (16- to 33-foot) waves pounded Williston Lake at times, even threatening the ferries. The visibility in the lake was limited to 3 metres (10 feet), so after the tugboat was found, four dives were required to secure four lines to it. As expected, the bottom was mud and debris at a depth of 14 metres (46 feet). As was usually the case, the boat was brought up without further difficulty. Another mission accomplished.

I certainly would not have wanted to take the dive Russ made in August 1970. The site was the effluent lagoon at a pulp mill in Prince George. Prior to the dive the effluent was checked for caustic content

and a reading of 7.4 was attained. Because of this, Russ had to cover his face and exposed skin with a barrier cream. After the dive he also had to undergo a complete hose-down. An additional cost of $130 was assessed for a new rubber suit and accessories because they were partly consumed by the caustic effluent.

Submerging into the effluent lagoons was a fairly common event. Russ recalls the time a fellow diver

Russ Logan emerges from the effluent pond on a safety rope.

The effluent lagoons at the pulp mills are so caustic that a diver has to cover and protect every inch of skin.

was preparing to enter the lagoon when Russ advised him to cover all of his exposed skin, including his fancy handlebar mustache. The gentleman ignored the advice and, after emerging from the lagoon, found himself the bearer of some powerful odours. That evening after he had scrubbed himself thoroughly, he crawled into bed with the desire to have a bit of loving. One sniff by his ever-loving was enough for her to advise him that either the mustache or he had to go. The end result was that the fancy mustache, which had been tended with such love and affection, was cut off and flushed down the drain. Russ kidded his chum that he should consider patenting what could be a new form of birth control.

In Russ Logan's line of work he never knew what to expect, such as on October 28, 1970, when he drove about 70 kilometres (42 miles) to a camp on Trembleur Lake. A barge had tipped and dropped its load of contents into 7 metres (23 feet) of water, and he was hired to bring all the cargo to the surface. In the limited visibility, this required three dives over a period of two hours just to find the main loss. One handy item that was used in the search was a strong magnet; this helped locate metal goods hidden in the mud.

Not all dives met with instant success. Russ was called to Raspberry Harbour at Williston Lake on December 11, 1970. A dozer boat and tractor had gone down in 35 metres (115 feet) of water and it was hoped that they could be towed to shore. The tugboat being used had churned up an enormous amount of mud and silt, and with the poor visibility they were unable to find the tractor. A poly line with a buoy was attached to the tugboat so that it could be located after the ice went off the lake. Both items were later recovered with a barge and crane.

On February 12, 1971, Russ and a co-diver made their way to Blackwater Camp on Williston Lake. Their target was a sunken barge that was

Dozer boat.

hanging suspended from a log boom. Visibility was limited to half a metre (less than 2 feet). Russ's diary reads:

> 1. Six dives were made to attach lines to barge hanging
> suspended from log boom. Top of barge in 5 metres [16
> feet] of water. Extremely dangerous due to conditions.
> 2. Seven dives were made to remove cables and "bub-
> bling" manifold from barge and suspend on barrels (for
> floatation). Only two of four systems were located.
> 3. Dove to over 30 metres [100 feet] to locate compressor
> that had tipped off the barge. Compressor was found to
> be upside down, so I was unable to determine if bubbling
> manifold was attached to compressor. Attached cable to
> cross member of wooden skid on bottom of compressor.

The job was completed successfully, but this was not anyone's
idea of a fun job. The water temperature under the ice was 1°C (34°F).

In January Russ was called to Williston Lake where a 404 Timberjack
and truck had fallen through the ice and gone to the bottom in over 30
metres (100 feet) of water. One dive was required to attach a cable to the
rear axle and place a buoy on it so it could be found later. After the ice
went off the lake, the equipment was lifted aboard a barge.

In June Russ and co-divers Al Shaw and Dick Wood were back at Raspberry Harbour for the third time. This time they were to retrieve a dozer boat and tractor from 10 metres (33 feet) of water. Lines were attached to the dozer boat, which in turn was attached to the tractor. Both were raised successfully.

Some jobs were a little out of Russ's line of expertise, such as the time he was called to Stuart Lake and the Stuart River outlet. Columbia Airlines needed 46 pilings removed as they were a constant threat to aircraft landing and taking off from the river. On the first dive, two pilings were dynamited and removed as a test run. On the second dive, five pilings were removed; on the third, all remaining 39 pilings were blown and the job completed.

An innovative concept was put to the test on Williston Lake. It comprised a floating camp complete with dozer boats and a crane. The dozer boats would move the floating trees to the crane, which would then bundle and transport them to a dewatering device that lifted them out of the water to a mill or to a yard where they were loaded on trucks for transport. The enormous number of floating trees kept the camp in operation for several years. On occasion Russ and his assistants were called to this camp to retrieve objects lost in the debris-strewn lake, such as a dozer boat that turned turtle and sank.

Imagine working in among trees, stumps and mud 18 metres (60 feet) beneath the surface of Williston Lake. The bubbling system that was used to keep the lake free of ice for the ferry transporting truckloads of logs across the lake during the winter had failed. It required a total of 14 dives over two days to find and replace the broken lines, which were brought to the surface and replaced. In all cases the tee fittings were broken. The date was December 19, 1971. A week later Russ and his crew were back to repair the broken lines again. Apparently the bubbling system left much to be desired, because on January 7 they were back again to find that a reducer had failed.

A friend of mine took a scuba diving course from Russ Logan and assured me that he was an excellent instructor. In fact, he taught instructors and built up an enviable reputation in the diving world. One day I became the victim of some diving humour, an incident that took place because of my indulgence in the sport of ice fishing. My buddy Dan Schlitt and I were debating world affairs while ice fishing in Cluculz Lake west of Prince George when we were rudely interrupted by the sound of a chainsaw just a stone's throw away. In due course it stopped, and a short time later I felt a mighty tug on my fishing line. I hauled it in only to find the bait had not been disturbed. Again I put the line down and another tug produced the same result—no fish and no damage to the bait. This defied logic, as the bait was barely attached to the hook. I was in deep conversation with Dan trying to determine what was happening when another solid tug hit my line. This time I hauled it out only to find I had a cup on my

Playing ice hockey.

hook. Suddenly the lights came on and I realized that some divers were training just a short distance away. One of them, an acquaintance named Neil Miller, had detoured over our way to play a joke on me. Attached to the others by a rope, he swam under the ice to place a cup on my fish hook. If Neil's intentions had been to surprise me, he certainly got his money's worth, as he had me going for a time there.

For Russ and his co-divers, some trips were not much more than a ride to and from the site, such as the trip to Williston Lake in May 1972. Fellow diver Dave went underwater to inspect the propeller and shaft of the tugboat *Peace Prince*. A simple dive into 2 metres (6.5 feet) of water and he found the problem: 8 metres (26 feet) of poly rope was wrapped around the propeller and shaft, plus a few sticks were caught in the cage. A few minutes' work with a knife and hacksaw and it was all systems go.

⚓

Some trips were worth their weight in the adventures and sightseeing alone. May 1972 found Russ and co-diver Al Shaw at the Pelly and Liard rivers. The dives were made for Water Surveys of Canada at Faro to install two nitrogen bubbling systems, one on the Pelly River at Faro and the other on the Liard River at Mile 496 Alaska Highway. Four man-days of diving and four man-days of standby were required to complete the operation. The end result, including airfare, accommodations and meals, was a bill for $1,379.75.

Russ was out on several local calls to area pulp mills and then on June 12 he was called to Chinaman Creek at Williston Lake. A T.D. 20 crawler tractor had fallen into 12 metres (40 feet) of water. Working in zero visibility, the divers found and attached cables to the unit so that it could be lifted out and recovered.

Perhaps the strangest dive of Russ's career occurred at Tabor Lake near Prince George for an insurance firm. The purpose of the dive was to recover a diamond ring that had somehow dropped into 2 metres (6.5 feet) of water. Russ rented a metal detector and then spent three hours on the lake bottom, where he recovered a lot of debris such as tin cans and metal foil. The ring was not found.

The front-end loader lifted out of Six-Mile Lake.

During late January 1974 a $35,000 front-end loader was clearing snow off Six-Mile Lake in preparation for the coming winter carnival when it broke through the ice. The owners, R.F. Klein and Sons, were anxious to get it out and back to work as quickly as possible. Russ and co-diver Bruce Pease went to the site and made a chainsaw cut in the ice from the shore to the hole where the loader had fallen through. Several large barrels were taken out to the spot.

Next, a trail of dynamite was placed under the ice beneath the saw cut. After the explosives made a clear break in the ice, the barrels were sunk, attached to the loader and then filled with compressed air. This allowed the loader to rise off the bottom, and then a tractor pulled it to shore.

During the operation the loader shifted position and came down on Russ, trapping him. He signalled to his partner, Bruce, who promptly brought a spare tank down to him and assisted in digging him out. The final act was when the loader was lifted out

Russ carrying the dynamite at Six-Mile Lake.

of the water by a crane. A rather unusual dive but effective nonetheless. Even the operator's lunch box and an apple were recovered from the lake bed.

So it should be no surprise that Roni only learned of her husband's close call 20 years later, after he had retired from diving.

Some jobs were a steal, financially speaking, such as the time Russ dove at Williston Lake to retrieve a D7 crawler tractor for contractor Al Thorell. Once again a machine had been lost off a barge, but only one dive was required and a line was secured to the winch of the tractor. It was then brought to the surface. A small cost indeed when one considers the value of the machine involved.

Burning off fuel before a dive.

When I queried Russ about them setting fire to the lake, he told me that a tanker truck had broken through the ice and it was necessary to burn off the fuel before diving. This prevented getting any diesel burns on exposed flesh. It also prevented contaminating the lake.

✦

A tragic situation brought Russ and co-diver Kerry Gibbons to Northwood Pulp Mill in Prince George when two men were lost in the effluent pond. Working in zero visibility, the divers found one of the victims but had to admit defeat on finding the second because of the danger of becoming entangled in lines hanging from a barge.

Imagine being called to Williston Lake and asked to dive under an ice bridge at -40°C (-40°F). The dives had to be aborted because the lines and tanks in their breathing apparatus were constantly freezing up.

The difficulty involved in working in fast water was shown again and again. A chip car was lost in the Fraser River where the water was running fast and furious. The divers were unable to locate it as it had rolled, possibly far down the river. In a similar situation, a 4-metre (14-foot) boat was lost and the search was aborted; in that case the boat may have gone all the way to the ocean.

The number of call-outs to pulp mills because of silt buildup was astounding. In fact, probably over half of the call-outs were of this nature. Time and again the men dove into darkness or had to work inside pipes below water level.

During September 1978 Russ and fellow diver Al Shaw were hired by the Insurance Corporation of BC to drive to beautiful Muncho Lake where a truck and trailer had left the highway and disappeared into the depths. The driver managed to escape, but the co-driver never had a chance. He was fast asleep in the sleeper behind the cab when the truck entered the water. Cables were attached to the truck, trailer and trailer wheels, and all were brought back into the light of day. A great amount of damage was incurred by the cab of the truck when it hit the water at what must have been high speed.

Always looking for a bit of humour, Russ recalls the time he and a friend went out on a navy ship off Hawaii. The purpose of the trip was to dive down to a sunken submarine 40 metres (130 feet) underwater. Both men acted like novices and had the chief diver in turmoil when they returned with most of their air still in the tanks. The head honcho wouldn't let them go until they admitted that they were professionals who had taken special training in breathing.

Another escapade was putting some garlic into the filter of a friend's scuba gear. He couldn't detect it but everyone else could. Revenge was sweet for that gentleman because, being a policeman, he nailed Russ and company for coroner's duty every chance he got.

Training divers was not all work by any means. These men invented their own games, which were played underwater. It seems to me that teaching divers to concentrate on other things as well as diving would improve their ability to perform in a pinch. It was not a piece of cake to become a certified diver; Russ assures me that not all people passed, in spite of giving them every opportunity to do so.

When I asked Russ how deep he had gone underwater, Northwood slide.

he related a dive along the Marianna Wall off Powell River to 67 metres (220 feet). He and a co-diver were just blissfully allowing themselves to sink and didn't realize how far down they had gone. When I questioned him about getting "the bends" (nitrogen bubbles in the blood) he told me that several of them had deliberately got the bends just to experience the phenomenon, which he described as comparable to knives slicing into your body.

Some accidents are rather hard to explain, such as the skidder that fell off the railway bridge in Prince George. It seems apparent that the low-bed carrying the skidder must have struck a steel girder on the bridge, forcing the machine over into the river. A Cat was brought to the scene and a diver managed to locate the skidder in the dirty river water — no easy task when we realize that visibility is restricted to zero when the river runs high.

Just as there is another world of beauty and wonder high in the mountains, so is there a similar world beneath the waves, a world of stunning beauty and amazing creatures. Russ told how he watched the other denizens of the deep, and if he noticed them leaving the area en masse, he would leave as well because this meant danger was approaching. One day a giant sea lion swam up and looked him right in the eye through his mask, turned and swam away.

Bubbling system in use at Williston Lake.

D8 Cats at Williston Lake.

In order to prevent many unnecessary miles of hauling, logging companies set up a bubbling system in Williston Lake. This kept ice off an open lane so that ferries could cross with loaded logging trucks throughout the winter months. This was just one of countless ideas that were utilized in the Williston area. Ice bridges were also used, but low speed limits were enforced because a wave could form ahead of a speeding truck, which could cause the ice to break. A great number of trucks, Cats and other equipment was recovered by divers, a pittance when compared to the value of the equipment. An example was a D8 Cat that was brought to the edge of the lake to recover a D8 Cat already underwater. The bank broke away and the second D8 Cat had to be rescued as well.

A bit of courage must have been called for on the day Russ went down into the Fraser River at Shelley, about 25 kilometres (15 miles) upriver of Prince George. The jack-ladder chain that brings logs up into the mill had jammed and a dive was required to find the problem. Russ had to work completely by feel in the murky water. The problem turned out to be a waterlogged piece of tree that had settled on the bottom and jammed the chain. Again working by feel, he attached a line to it and it was pulled out, allowing the mill to continue operation.

Russ was often called upon by the police and, all told, was involved in the recovery of 23 bodies. A special memory that has stayed with him

Russ prepares to dive into the Fraser River at Shelley Sawmills.

was the time he went into the water with a killer whale at the Seattle Aquarium. He swam around it and repeatedly tried to touch it. The animal would not allow it, and after several attempts it swung its tail right up against his face. It didn't hurt him, but he got the message and left it alone after that warning.

Russ looks back on a fairly successful career, but sometimes success was impossible — such as the time they dove into the Fraser River looking for a missing bridge. Nothing was found, demonstrating once again the power of water. Or how about the time a set of tire tracks stopped at the riverbank in Fort George Park? Several dives were made, but no trace of a vehicle was ever found. Possibly the divers were within an arm's length of the vehicle but were unable to see it in the murky water; it is also possible that the vehicle is in the Pacific Ocean somewhere. In retrospect, Russ describes it as an exciting and profitable means of earning a livelihood, especially considering it just started out as a hobby.

2

Along the Salmon Streams

There is something in human nature that demands adventure and excitement; some people cannot settle for less. One such gentleman is a chap named Leon Lorenz. A wildlife filmmaker, he has put out a number of videos under the name Canadian Wildlife Productions. Of the videos he has produced so far, my favourite is *Sheep and Grizzly Country*. This is some of the best photography of wild grizzlies ever to come to my attention. It is available at www.wildlifevideos.ca.

Mike Lorenz and children. Photo Leon Lorenz.

But what lit the light for Leon that caused him to lead such a life? Let's pull up a chair and take heed as he gives a brief description of his childhood and the reasons for the life he chose to follow:

It was September 1959 when my parents loaded us children and their possessions into their International pickup truck and moved to Dunster in the Robson Valley east of McBride, BC. Dad had enough of operating a paving machine in Alberta, so he purchased 160 acres of land in this beautiful valley; his desire was to raise cattle and a family. On one side of this lush valley stood the mighty Rocky Mountains; on the opposite side, the Cariboo Mountains.

I was two years of age when we arrived at Dunster and I remember the tall grass surrounding the buildings. I also recall what happened the next morning when we watched a large bull moose browsing at the edge of our clearing. Without a licence or tag, Dad was forced to pass up our winter supply of meat. We never got another chance at a moose so we went the entire winter without wild game to supplement our diet. It must have been tough on our parents with five little children to care for. They ended up having seven children in seven years and they raised us without electricity or running water. If we wanted running water, we had to take a pail to the well and then run back with it.

My older brother and I followed Dad's example in trapping and hunting. The extra dollars we earned from the furs helped us purchase outdoor supplies. Dad was an excellent hunter and a crack shot with his .308 rifle. He brought home many moose, deer and other game as well. Two of the moose he shot stand out vividly in my memory: one summer a cow moose took great pleasure in eating our cabbages and other staples, until Dad decided to add her to our menu. He fired one shot and dropped her with a cabbage leaf still in her mouth.

The other moose memory took place the year Dad hunted long and hard without any success. Moose were not always easy to get. We desperately needed the meat, and when Dad decided to give it one more try, Mom called all us children into the house and asked us to pray that Dad would get a moose. We took turns saying a prayer and before we finished we heard a shot toward the river. Dad had shot a fine bull moose and our prayers were truly answered. We had no other means of preserving the meat back then so Mom canned all of it in two-quart jars. Every year we planted a large garden near the house and this kept our family fed.

Hunting ruffed grouse was a big thing for me. If I managed to bag several of them with my Winchester single-shot .22 rifle, the feast was on. When a platter of them was passed around the table and handed to me first, a warm feeling came over me; I felt I was contributing something of value. One fall day I got a grouse and was searching for more when I spotted a great horned owl eyeing me from its perch about 15 feet [4.5 metres] up in a tree. I threw the grouse high up in the air and in the blink of an eye the owl left its perch and dove at the bird in midair. Just before it grabbed the bird I shouted and frightened it enough that it went back to its perch in the tree. As I look back 40 years as a wildlife filmmaker, I wish I would have let the owl take the bird, just for observation purposes.

Trapping was an important part of our childhood for my brother and me. We caught mink, marten, ermine, squirrels and lynx, which we sold to the raw fur auctions. We used to check our traps once every week, and "Our lucky day," as we call it, was the time we caught 13 mink and marten. We skinned our catch by lamplight in the living room and I recall our sisters telling us not to cut the scent glands of the mink. They did not like the strong smell.

The highlight of those years was when I caught six lynx, among other furs, one winter. From the sale money I saved enough to buy a Honda Trail 90 motorcycle.

Times sure have changed over the past 40 years. When I was a teenager I walked alone into a pawn shop in Edmonton and bought a .22 rifle. Then I walked several blocks to where Dad had his truck parked. I never got a second look from anyone. Another time I took my .22 rifle to high school, minus the stock, so the shop teacher could help me install a scope side-mount on it. I also carried it on the school bus and no one questioned me, not even the teachers.

Growing up on the farm involved a lot more than hunting and trapping. Work such as milking and feeding cows, fixing fences, chopping wood, gardening and picking wild berries were just some of the many chores that needed to be done. My mother told me that from an early age I held a keen interest in nature and often watched small creatures such as birds, snakes and frogs. When I was about nine years old my teacher showed a film on beavers. Even at that young age I felt a desire to make films of wildlife. About 25 years later that dream came true and the year 2010 marks 19 years of filmmaking for me. Praise God for everything.

Leon Lorenz at work.
Photo Leon Lorenz.

Leon spends a vast amount of time in the high country and along salmon streams in order to capture his priceless footage. One image that stands out on his sheep and grizzly video has a grizzly walking right up to him along the bank of a river, and only when it is a few yards away does he finally say, "That's close enough!" I had already made the decision for him several seconds earlier.

Since it is perfectly obvious from his videos that he is having continual close encounters with grizzly bears, I asked for a few of his most memorable recollections. He obliged with the following:

> I was hip-wading along the Torpy River in search of chinook salmon spawning and hopefully a hungry grizzly or two. The weather was quite hot and I had worked up a good sweat carrying my camera equipment. When I came to a good filming location, I stripped off all my sweaty clothes and hung them up to dry. With unscented soap I took a quick cold-water bath and then stood in my birthday suit on the riverbank beside my tripod-mounted camera, watching for wildlife. After a short while I heard what sounded like a salmon splashing close to shore. The brush grew right tight to the shoreline and I was about 2 yards [1.8 metres] up the riverbank, so I couldn't see what was coming around the river bend so close to shore. Suddenly a grizzly appeared right in front of me

Bear with chinook salmon. Photo Leon Lorenz.

and about 6 yards [5.5 metres] away. My first thought was "Should I try to film or reach for my .44 Magnum revolver?" which was still in the holster near my pack on the ground. I decided to turn the camera on, start the recording and then reach for the gun. I knew the bear had caught my scent, however, it didn't know where I was, and it was possible it could charge up the bank right into me. With the camera recording the bear, I slowly turned and reached for my gun. This slow movement and possibly slight sound alerted the grizzly and it quickly spun around and ran back a few yards, then charged right up the bank and was gone. Imagine if it had charged directly at me; it would have been upon me before the gun cleared the holster, that's for certain. The footage of the event has turned out awesome and hopefully will appear in my future film *Wildest of the Wild.*

Because of the close-up pictures Leon has to get, he has had several interesting moments with the creatures of the forest, and it was only after

Dave Wirtz at the campfire. Photo Leon Lorenz.

some of these events took place that he realized it was incumbent upon him to carry a firearm before, rather than after, a tragedy took place.

One of Leon's favourite stories concerns the time in 1984 when he and a friend went hunting grizzlies. The bears were not in any danger, but not so for the hunters.

I never did have a burning desire to hunt grizzly bears, but my friend Dave Wirtz did. At the time I was on holidays because the sawmill where I had been employed had temporarily closed. It was spring breakup, so Dave was also on lay-off. He called and asked if I wanted to join him on a McGregor River grizzly bear hunt. I told him, "Sure, it sounds like a great idea." Back then, getting a grizzly tag was as easy as walking into a sports shop and buying one.

At the time I owned a .280 Remington with maximum hand-load and 175-grain Nosler bullets, so I felt I was prepared for the hunt. Dave also felt confident with the .270 Winchester he was using. It didn't take long for us to throw some gear and grub together and away we went in Dave's 4x4 pickup, heading into the McGregor River watershed. Dave had spent time logging in the valley so the area was familiar to him. Due to the time of year, known as breakup, the roads were still soft, so it wasn't long until we had to park the truck, shoulder our packs and rifles, and head off walking. We walked for about four hours, glassing all the slides as we went; unfortunately, all the best slides were on the other side of the river. By mid-afternoon we were hiking along the shore of the river, well beyond the end of the logging road.

I don't remember who spotted the grizzlies first, but across the river, high up on a mountain slide, two grizzlies were feeding on the new vegetation. It looked like a sow accompanied by a huge boar that looked as big as a horse. Up to this point the hiking had been fairly easy, but crossing the river, which had risen from the recent rains and melting snow, was the challenge. We searched in vain

Leon rafting the McGregor River.

for a crossing spot and then decided to fall a tree to span the river. We found one about 20 inches [50 centimetres] in diameter and Dave attacked it with his little hatchet, the only tool in our possession. We took turns chopping the tree and watching the bears through our binoculars. The head of the hatchet kept coming loose so after each few chops we had to thump it against the tree to tighten it up again. Chop, chop, thump, was the rhythm, over and over again. An hour later, with one person chopping and the other pushing with a long pole, the tree was ready to drop. Right then we heard what sounded like a motorboat coming up the river; this scared us because the tree could have fallen on the boat. Thankfully, whatever it was, it never got to us. We settled down and with a few more chops, and a mighty push, the tree dropped across the river. It hit the water with a mighty splash, and to our dismay landed about 10 feet [3 metres] short of the opposite bank. The powerful current caught the branches and slowly our hard-won footbridge went down the river.

Left with no other option, we had to build a raft. We had passed an old sawmill site just a short distance downriver, so we hiked back to the spot. We found four suitable logs, which we manoeuvred into place, and luckily we found boards with nails in them, which we pulled for use on the raft. By morning we had finished building the raft and were ready for a wild river crossing. We shoved off with our poles, intent on hitting the gravel bar on the opposite bank. It didn't work out though, as our heavy raft had a mind of its own in the powerful river current. Although we pushed with all our strength, it soon became apparent that we were not going to make the intended landing spot on the other bank. By this point we were in the fastest, deepest part of the river, heading around a bend 10 feet [3 metres] from shore when Dave shouted, "Should we jump?"

I shouted back, "No! Just hang on!"

As soon as we rounded the bend, the river widened and split into two channels. Then our raft grounded out in the middle of the river. We tried with all our might but we could not get it moving again. With no other option, we abandoned ship. We threw our hiking boots across and then waded the 40 feet [12 metres] to shore through waist-deep water in the powerful current.

For the next two days we hunted the slides, hoping to find a grizzly; in particular, the big boar we had spotted earlier. But the weather had warmed and the bears

Bighorn sheep in paradise. Photo Leon Lorenz.

40   BOUDREAU

had moved away. With our food running low we had no choice but to call off the hunt.

For the return river crossing we decided to build a much smaller raft, using two smaller logs and a lot of cross pieces from another mill-site on shore. When the raft was completed we pushed off and quickly found that the raft would not support our weight. It sank about one and a half feet [half a metre] below the water level, then levelled off and fortunately carried us across without swamping. This surely would have made the World's Funniest Videos: two men crossing the river with no raft in sight. We didn't manage to get a bear on this hunt, but we sure got some wonderful, humorous memories.

At a fairly young age Leon had already experienced his share of adventures in the woods, so perhaps it should be no surprise that he became a wildlife filmmaker. In among his videos is some fantastic footage of bighorn mountain sheep, which was filmed in stunning scenery high in the mountains. In one instance he filmed a lone ram that attempted to join a family of sheep that included three mature rams. This started a fight that lasted for several hours. Leon named the lone ram Stranger because he was unknown to the other rams, but he also could have picked that name because he responded in a rather strange way. Time after time the other rams charged him and he fought back gallantly. Often two rams would attack in rapid succession, but Stranger held his own. Only after

Hummingbirds. Photo Leon Lorenz.

hours had passed and he had received an injury near his right eye did the newcomer slowly wander away. In retrospect, he could well have been named Courage.

I think I have watched Leon's videos at least ten times and I'm not finished yet. It is what I have spent much of my life doing and loving—studying wildlife around timberline in the mountains. Since health problems have curtailed my hiking ability, I will let Leon do the footwork and I will enjoy the finished product.

Leon warns people about hanging around logjams when salmon are running the rivers, and it may be wise to follow his advice. These spots are places where dying and dead salmon hang up, therefore the grizzlies frequent these areas. Leon has been within a few metres of grizzlies in these locations and has the photographic proof. Discretion is the better part of valour when these bears are after salmon. They are stocking up fat for the long winter months and may well resent people interfering with their salmon catch. Leon explains that these grizzlies can pick up the smell of a salmon lying in the bottom of a pool. As proof, he shows a sow with a cub walk down a logjam, put her head under the water and come up with a dead salmon. It seems apparent that she knew where the salmon was before she went down the jam because she went straight to it.

Some of the pictures Leon has accumulated show that he has enormous patience and will spend days waiting for wildlife to get into the right positions. No doubt patience is the most important asset while filming wildlife and eventually pays huge dividends.

When I was just a lad I heard stories of wolves attempting to catch salmon, and a wildlife photographer has confirmed that not only do they try to catch them, they succeed. While following a salmon stream in Alaska, he got good footage of a wolf successfully taking one, and a large one at that. Perhaps the wolves watch bears as they catch salmon and decide that they can do the same thing. Leon has close-up pictures of wolves following salmon streams. Should they be successful, I imagine one large chinook salmon would be enough sustenance to last a wolf for several days. However, I suspect that the wolves do not have to catch their own salmon; they must do quite well just picking up scraps after the bears have taken their fill of the choicest parts.

In all the years I spent studying grizzlies in the mountains, not once did I catch them in the act of copulation, yet Leon has been lucky or tenacious enough to catch this on video several times. I believe the main reason for his success is that he spends a lot of time on the job in late June and early July. I generally missed those months, and spent the months of April and May around the bears. Again, I was back after them in the last part of July and then August, September and October, weather permitting. I did have more luck with black bears; I caught them mating many times.

In his DVD *Journey Home of the Chinook Salmon,* Leon and his guests describe the life cycles of these salmon in great detail. Their return to the headwaters of the Fraser River is an ordeal beyond imagination. It is small wonder that they lose up to 30 percent of their body weight. Since they do not eat after they reach fresh water, they often end up travelling on heart alone. I have seen them almost all white and at the edge of death when they arrive at their spawning site. Truthfully, they appear to be travelling on nothing but willpower.

I love to watch eagles along the salmon streams. Sometimes they take part of a salmon and fly away to land in a tree where they devour part of their catch. The reason I say "part of their catch" is because they often drop parts of the fish as they dine. These bits fall to the forest floor where a host of other creatures get their turns at the dinner table. Leon has a great deal of footage of eagles. They sure can put on a performance when several of them get together along a salmon stream or on a carcass. It is really something to watch them grab a salmon with their talons and try to bring it to shore. They beat their wings this way and that in an effort to keep their balance. The times that I have seen bald eagles go into the water—once because of a fight with another eagle—they had to swim to shore using their wings as oars. After witnessing this, I assumed that eagles could not rise up out of the water after they got their wing feathers wet.

Grizzly looking for salmon. Photo Leon Lorenz.

Leon has made me change my mind. He has photographic proof of a bald eagle fighting a chinook salmon for some time and, in the process, getting its feathers wet. At least, they must have been wet because the bird was pulled underwater. When the eagle finally gave up, it rose out of the water with apparent ease. I stand corrected, but at the same time I wonder why the other eagles had to swim to shore. Leon assures me that if an eagle grabs a salmon by the head, it can release its talons quite easily; however, if it grabs the soft underbelly it will have a harder time letting go.

Sometimes the eagles get fooled by an exceptionally large salmon. My friend Doug Cameron watched an eagle dive on a salmon in the Skeena River near Prince Rupert and what a show it turned out to be. The fish took the eagle under the surface of the water, and for some reason the bird was unable to let go of the fish. When it did finally free itself, it had a terrible time splashing its way to a nearby boom. The last view Doug got was the eagle with one wing up on the boom; then it slipped beneath the water and did not reappear.

Leon has had some surprises while watching and filming eagles:

> The rarest bald eagle footage I ever saw and managed to capture occurred when I was filming waterfowl in early spring for my movie *Feathered Friends*. I was crouched in a blind, filming near an opening in the ice where Canada geese were landing. A pair of geese took off and I was panning along with them when I heard excited honking. I quickly panned the camera back to the open water and there was a large, immature bald eagle trying to grab a goose by the neck. The attack didn't stand much of a chance, as the goose's mate put up such a loud ruckus that the eagle gave up and decided to hunt elsewhere.

Leon's other eagle story certainly brought back memories for me.

> This story took place when I was working on my second film, *Mountain Wonders*. I had climbed up near the top of a mountain when I stopped for a rest. I began glassing the surrounding area and picked up a wolverine running down a steep ridge. It was pursued by a golden eagle,

which repeatedly dive-bombed it, each time pulling up about 6 feet [2 metres] above it. I took my camera out of my pack and set it on the tripod, but I was about five seconds too late. I guess the eagle had decided not to push its luck or tease any further. I didn't manage to capture the dives, but I did manage to get some good footage of the wolverine looking back toward the eagle.

This story held great significance for me, because I saw a similar fight between a wolverine and an osprey in an outdoor film. The film started with the wolverine climbing a dead snag, heading for an osprey's nest on the top. As it neared the top, the osprey started diving right into the animal. Each time, just as it was about to strike, the wolverine would release one paw from the tree and strike at the bird, and each time a small cloud of feathers would float down from the bird. After several dives the osprey gave up and retreated. The wolverine continued to the top of the snag and feasted.

I wonder if Leon happened to stumble into a similar situation. Perhaps the wolverine had attempted to get at the eagle's nest only to have

Family of black bears. Photo Leon Lorenz.

the eagle dive-bomb it. There is a considerable difference between the size of an eagle and an osprey. The eagle may well have been able to knock the wolverine clean out of the tree and then pursue it for good measure.

Ruffed grouse. Photo Leon Lorenz.

Another interesting point made by Leon is that in the eight years he spent getting information and video about salmon, not once did he find golden eagles feeding along the upper Fraser River. This seems to support what I have always believed, that the closer you are to lakes and rivers, the more apt you are to find bald eagles. Alternatively, the farther you get from lakes and rivers, the more likely you will find golden eagles.

It is impossible for a person to spend many years in the woods and not have unusual adventures. Leon shared the following experience with me, and I agree it was definitely different:

When it comes to filming wildlife you try to expect the unexpected. On a filming trip I came across a family of coyote pups located at the base of a pile of old logs. I was able to get some intimate footage of the pups playing by setting up my camera about 25 metres [82 feet] away with a camouflage cover over me. The following day I returned to the site intent on catching the mother bringing some freshly caught prey to her growing youngsters. Before long I heard some very excited yapping and barking made by a coyote coming towards the den site. My first thought was that she had detected my scent and was seriously upset. I found it strange that her yapping seemed to be switching from one side of the forest to the other, but her yapping grew louder as I intently watched the thick bush ahead of me. By this time her pups had disappeared into her den. Imagine my surprise when four large brown bears came clambering over the log pile to the den site. My first thought was grizzlies, but I quickly realized they were not grizzlies but huge brown black bears, a mother with her three nearly full-grown offspring. The excited mother coyote had evidently been trying to lure these bears away from the den site. The coyote continued yapping and pacing back and forth as the bears carefully checked out the den entrance. On more than one occasion the bears charged the mother coyote, and at one point the coyote ran towards me and came within 20 feet [6 metres] of me with a bear chasing her. Eventually the mother bear caught my scent, stood on her hind legs for a while, then took off fast with her family. For three minutes I had managed to film this rare event taking place in nature.

Leon was indeed lucky to be so close to such a rare event. I guess if you spend enough time out there you are bound to luck out sooner or later. Here is another of Leon's strange experiences:

Several years ago I was on a moose-filming trip to the Muskwa area of northern BC when my filming ended abruptly. The weather was unusually hot for September so I chose to film high in the mountains. For about a week I managed to get some action of moose rutting. Late one evening I was glassing a distant beaver pond down in a small valley about a mile away when I spotted two moose head to head in combat. Several other moose, which I believed were cows, stood around them in the pond area. Next morning I decided to leave the high country and move my spike camp down into this valley close to the beaver ponds.

Over the next several days I managed to film a number of moose including an average-sized bull. Each morning I positioned myself at a good vantage point watching for any incoming moose. On this particular morning nothing showed up so I headed over a ridge and down into a swampy area. Almost immediately I spotted five cow moose and one of the most spectacular bulls I've ever seen. It had an average-sized rack, but its bell was probably 2 feet [60 centimetres] long. I managed to get some footage of the moose before they headed into heavy timber to spend the day. Late that evening they returned to the swampy area to drink. I was filming at about 50 yards [45 metres] when I heard the artificial call of a cow moose far off in the distance. I was sure it was a hunter, but I didn't think the bull was in any danger because the call sounded a long way off. The bull looked in the direction of the calls several times and was pacing back and forth a bit, but I knew he was not about to leave his harem of cows. Suddenly a gunshot rang through the little valley and I could see that the bull had taken a hit in the gut area. The shot had no immediate effect on the moose so the hunter continued to call. Another shot rang out. This time a front hoof was shot off and dangled by a piece of skin as the moose hobbled about. Sometime later two more shots rang out and the bull took a shot in the chest area. This held incredible potential for filming with this bull and his five cows, but it finally came to an end. While hiking back to camp late that evening I felt frustrated and angry about the poor shooting by that hunter.

That evening at 11 p.m. I was suddenly awakened by heavy moose steps coming directly to my small backpacking tent. I was camped in a small grove of trees and the moose evidently had wanted to pass through there. I yelled and caught the moose's attention so it wheeled around and crashed away. I believe if God hadn't awakened me to startle the moose, it may have gotten tangled in my tent and I could have been seriously injured or killed. That was the end of another exciting filming trip.

Throughout the 19 years that Leon spent filming wildlife he got close to bears countless times. So I was not surprised when he got into a serious argument with grizzlies. On June 16, 2010, I received an email from him. Just two days earlier he had what he described as the experience of a lifetime. As usual, he was in the process of hiking to an area where he hoped to get some grizzly video. But as it turned out, he got better video than he had bargained for. To put it mildly, a surprise was in store for him that day.

He was walking through a grassy area beside a stream, making little if any noise, when he came upon a mother and yearling grizzly eating vegetation, and only about 23 metres (75 feet) distant. He immediately started filming, but when the bears grazed in behind a tree, he had to move his camera a few feet in order to get clear of the lower branches of that tree. At that precise moment the sow looked up and saw him. Instantly she dove behind cover and made a circle, coming back toward Leon. Then once again she ran in a tight circle, and all the time she was making the steady huffing and puffing that bears are noted for. On the continuation of the second rush, the grizzly had decided to attack and came right around the tree. She was coming straight into Leon when he fired his handgun over her head at a distance of about 3 metres (10 feet). The instant the gun roared, the sow swerved to her left, then whirled and zigzagged her way out of sight. After the incredible shock of the attack, Leon still had the presence of mind to zoom in his camera to film part of the bears' retreat. Without doubt, when faced with a life or death situation, Leon has to be one of the coolest people ever to come to my attention.

The editor of the *Valley Sentinel,* Josh Estabrooks of McBride, BC, interviewed Leon and forwarded a copy to me. I thank Josh for his permission to reprint.

> On Monday, June 14, local filmmaker Leon Lorenz narrowly escaped a grizzly attack, and came away with the best footage of his entire life. The wildlife filmmaker has been out this spring getting footage of grizzly bear behaviour, and has been surprised at how many there are in the side valleys. "I've been filming them as much as I can for about a month, and I have been out almost every day. I have encountered at least ten different grizzlies—mothers with yearlings, mothers with two-year-olds, and some three-year-olds out on their own for the first time."
>
> Lorenz has been frequenting a spot in the Horsey Creek area where an avalanche across the road has acted

Leon faces a grizzly charge. Photo Leon Lorenz.

as a barrier for most of the season, isolating the bears from human contact. "Absolutely nobody has been back there because of the slide, which is why there are a lot of bears there."

The bear in question weighed in at over 400 pounds [over 180 kilograms] and had a two-year-old with her. "I filmed some real good stuff of them rubbing their backs on trees and crossing mountain streams; you get to know the bears after a while."

On this particular day, Lorenz headed out and immediately began seeing signs of bear activity. "I said to myself that I would be very surprised if I didn't see anything at all; little did I know how close I would actually get to them." Lorenz always packs a sidearm when he is out filming, as nature is unpredictable. "I always have my camera on the tripod with a camouflage cover over the back; when I come upon a subject, I set the tripod, level it, and duck under the cover so they don't see a human form."

The terrain where the bears were was more or less open, which made it easy to travel silently, a key component in catching candid bear activity. "I was walking along silently and suddenly I saw this large grizzly digging in the grass. I immediately set the camera up and ducked under the cover to begin filming. I had just started recording when she turned broadside to me, caught my scent, and looked directly at me."

Lorenz said that the series of events that followed occurred within 20 seconds, and if it hadn't been for his quick reflexes, he may not be here today to tell the story. "She disappeared for a few seconds to collect her two-year-old, and then she turned and started charging. She did a zigzag charge with her two-year-old right behind her. She was roaring and angry, but I was still filming; I hadn't even stood up yet."

Lorenz lost sight of the charging animals as they darted into the bushes. "I backed the camera out to wide angle and as I stood up, I pulled my handgun out. I didn't see her but I knew she was charging through the bushes. I fired my handgun and at the same instant she exploded out of the lower branches of this tree and the gun blast caught her in the face."

The footage shows the bear altering its path slightly, most likely the result of the gunshot, which stopped the two-year-old in its tracks. The mother bear's momentum carried her right past Lorenz, who grabbed his camera to catch her as they ran off together. "She

This grizzly got a little too close for comfort. Photo Leon Lorenz.

was using the tree as a shield; it wasn't a straight charge. The two-year-old was doing exactly what she was doing, which indicates she was teaching it. It followed her every move; when she attacked, it attacked."

During the 19 years he has been filming in the woods, this is the first time he has had to fire his gun. After the bears took off, he immediately watched the footage and checked the ground to make sure he hadn't hit her. "I went back to check to see if I hit her for my own peace of mind. From watching the footage I know I missed her, but a split second earlier or later, either I would have been dead or the mother bear would have been dead."

Lorenz said that when he returned home the emotions of the experience started to sink in. "When I got home it was very emotional. We didn't get to bed until midnight. The boys were crying, and the wife and I had to have them in our bed for a while. I slept for about an hour and a half and then I woke up and couldn't get back to sleep for hours."

He said that he will have to work himself up to go back into the woods with his camera, but he is confident he will soon return to the same level of comfort he has experienced throughout his long career as a wildlife filmmaker. "I have never ever seen this type of footage before; there have been cases of bear attacks documented over the years, but who gets the chance to have it on camera? I have the whole thing on high definition, and I am thankful to be able to hug my children and my wife; it puts things in perspective."

Lorenz's company, Canadian Wildlife Productions, is working on a collection of some of the most exciting moments in the wilderness. It is aptly titled "Wildest of the Wild." It will be available in 2011. This experience, although not at all planned, will surely be included in the film. "I don't need anymore grizzly charges for this one," stated Lorenz [referring to his next DVD].

This week Lorenz was featured on CBC's The National and is in discussion with Global ... CTV, CBS, and a number of other news agencies to discuss his incredible ordeal.

People may wonder what made the mother bear abort her attack. Believe me when I say that these same people do not realize what it is like to be in front of a .44 Magnum when it is fired. It is a deafening sound that can make one's ears ring for several days. It is a shock that goes right through a person, so we can only imagine how it must hurt the sensitive ears of a bear. Leon says that he hand-loads his cartridges with 330-grain hard-cast bullets and maximum powder loads and has tested them by shooting through 30 centimetres (12 inches) of green poplar.

It was apparent that throughout the 20 or so seconds that the event covered, the young bear was right behind the mother, following her every move. It was also obvious that the bears used a bushy tree as a protective shield throughout most of the attack. The bears only fully exposed themselves when they burst around the tree and came at Leon.

After viewing the video of the attack many times, I am convinced that this was the bear's final rush. Leon was fortunate to have had his handgun with him; without it, I believe he would have been seriously mauled or killed. Take note that he deliberately shot high so the bears would not be injured.

To what do I attribute the reason for the charge? Grizzlies do not like to be surprised at close range—especially a mother with young. If mama thinks her young are in danger, then be prepared to defend yourself. Also take note that any hiker, or someone working in the woods, could have stumbled into that same situation. The difference is that they may not have been armed. As for meeting bears at close range, I would rather it be a big male than a mother with cubs. The lone bear only has to care for itself, therefore it does not feel the pressure experienced by a mother bear with young.

Speaking from experience, I know that grizzlies often make initial charges in an effort to determine what they are up against, and then they either attack or retreat. This does not apply to bears that have been wounded; in those cases you can bet their charges are for real.

This attack did not come as a complete surprise to me, because the close-up work Leon does with bears is not and cannot be without risk. The video of the attack was available all over the Web, but lately it seems to have disappeared. For those who have not seen it, it will be in Leon's next video, *Wildest of the Wild*. I look forward to it with much anticipation.

Obviously I am not the only one to acknowledge Leon's success. In 2007 and 2008 he won awards for *Journey Home of the Chinook Salmon* and *Sheep and Grizzly Country* at the International Film Festival in Missoula, Montana.

As to the risk Leon faces each day, there is no way to completely avoid risk in the work he does along salmon streams. Often thick brush grows along the waterways, which means that Leon can be right in among bears before he knows it. But let's look at the finished product. I fully support the years Leon has dedicated to gathering information about bears and their interrelationship with salmon. By the time I finished viewing *Journey Home of the Chinook Salmon*, I felt that I had a much clearer understanding of that relationship. Salmon are truly an integral part of nature and a precious resource that must be protected. It would warm my heart to see new areas opened for salmon spawning; and let's face it, there are so many possibilities.

⌐↓⌐

FOOTNOTE

Just as we were going to print with this book I got a rather interesting email from Leon Lorenz, who had just returned from filming grizzlies:

> Last week I spent five days filming the Walker Creek for grizzlies after salmon. I had about twelve encounters with four different grizzlies and I must share two grizzly encounters with the same bear about three hours apart. I'm set up with spawning salmon about 150 feet [45 metres] away across the river and watch all day for any passing bears to film. With no high riverbank to watch from, I'm forced to stand at water level. Suddenly without warning a large, lanky grizzly explodes from the bush

and into the water after the spawning salmon. I quickly turn the camera on and start the recording. The salmon scatter with the bear running here and there and he is really making the water fly. He then comes across to my shore and works his way along, checking out logs and such for any hung up spawned out salmon. At about 25 feet [8 metres] I pulled my gun out and was just going to say, "Close enough," when it sensed my presence and it wheeled and dashed high speed for the other side and into the bush, wow, what speed. However, in about two minutes it returned, sat down on the riverbank and started to scratch himself for a while before ambling away. Three hours later at about 8:15 p.m., it is quite low light now; I had just packed up my camera to hike back out when I heard a single snap of a branch break right behind me. I quickly grabbed my gun and stepped up onto the riverbank which was only 2 feet [60 centimetres] up from the river edge. At the same time a large grizzly rises to full height on his hind legs and at 20 feet [6 metres] from me with only some 4-foot-high [1.25 metres] brush between us. It towered much higher than I. With my gun sights aligned on his large neck I spoke softly, "It's okay." At the sound of my voice it dropped down to all fours, turned and was gone. I recognized it as the same one I had filmed earlier that day. Words really can't begin to describe what I had just experienced there in the fading light. The bear had chosen to follow the faint game trail on shore rather than the gravel bar as one would have expected it to. As I started to hike out 150 yards [137 metres] downstream from this encounter, I spotted a small grizzly speeding away as I approached on the gravel. At no time on these close encounters did I feel threatened. I believe many bears are shot when they stand up like this at close range because they are perceived as a bear in attack position. In reality they are just trying to see better.

3.

BETTY FRANK

There are still some people who believe women belong in the kitchen and not out in the woods running dog teams and pack horses, or chasing grizzly bears. But there are also some women who know better and readily set out to prove it. One such woman is Betty Frank, who went on to do just about every type of job in the woods, including several stints at guide/outfitting. Although this is just a brief look at her life, the entire story will be published by Caitlin Press in a year or so.

I first heard of Betty at a guide/outfitters' get-together, where it became apparent that here was a most unusual lady, well deserving of a place in posterity. In attempting to relate just a few of her adventures, I hope I don't stray too far off course. I didn't find it easy to interview Betty, as she is the only person I have ever known who can tell five different stories at the same time.

Many people probably remember the dance hall at the Williams Lake Stampede. Well, Betty was the person who started it. She ran it for several years until it was taken over by the city. It wasn't too long after that when things got totally out of hand. Beer bottles flying through the air became a regular form of entertainment. At times there was so much glass on the floor of the hall that it was impossible to dance.

About 1972 Betty started a band with two of her children and a friend. Aged 11 to 13, they may have been a little short on experience, but they made up for it with talent and got their start by winning a talent show in Prince George. Soon they were on the road travelling, and they managed to survive quite well with the money they earned playing music. But the highlight came when they were hired for a long stint on

Vancouver's Grouse Mountain. This gives just a little idea of the varied experiences in this woman's life.

One of the stories that preceded her trip to my home concerned a performance at a North Central Guide/Outfitters' Association annual meeting about 40 years ago. The highlight of the evening was Betty jumping out of a cake, clad in a fake grizzly hide with real claws and a real head. Paul Sissons, a Williams Lake taxidermist, created the bear suit. To add a touch of reality to the presentation, Don Peck of Fort St. John did a lot of roaring and growling. But the roaring came to a halt when Paul Sissons ran to her with his rifle and fired a pretend shot at this mad grizzly. Even more realism was added to the scene because the bear was foaming at the mouth, caused by the introduction of a can of shaving cream. In due course Betty collapsed and Paul pretended he was skinning her by removing the fake hide, which was held together with zippers. As if that wasn't enough, two game wardens in uniform rushed to her and started taking all her measurements to determine if she made the Boone and Crockett record book. The icing on the cake, so to speak, came when the hide was removed and out came Betty in a bikini complete with a Farrah Fawcett wig. At the same time the band was playing "When the Saints Go Marching In."

In spite of her antics in leopard bikinis and bearskins, Betty is an unusual and classy lady.

Many years have passed since that performance, but the memories have never faded. This was proven 17 years later when she performed a similar routine at a party in Prince George. Clad in panty hose with a leopard-skin top, she came out dancing and again brought the house down.

Dogs played an important part in Betty's life. She used them for trapping, racing and companionship. Throughout the years she sold hundreds of pups and bred some rather exotic types. Betty and two other people, trapper Tim Cushman and Jeff Dinsdale,

Betty on her horse Skipper, with her dog Yukon at her side.

Dog's played a big role in Betty's life. She used them for hunting and trapping, but she also bred and sold them to other guides and trappers.

each received two Greenland Eskimo dogs, which they thoroughly enjoyed. Their intent was to keep the breed going. These dogs had incredible stamina. They also had no hair under their paws, which meant they didn't develop ice balls that continually had to be removed on certain other breeds of dogs. Betty's experiment with these dogs ended badly when her bitch ran off and coaxed some of her other dogs away as well. The end result was that her dog had to be put down. Jeff had better luck with his two dogs and was successful in raising pups.

At one point during our interview a special memory caused Betty to break into laughter. She recalled the time she was heading north with a friend to attend dog races. Between the two of them, they had a total of over twenty dogs and four sleds in the back of a pickup. When they stopped at a café in Chetwynd for lunch, they allowed all the dogs out for a breath of fresh air. The result was that every window in the café was full of human faces. People could not believe the endless number of dogs that continued to stream out of that one vehicle.

The main problem with having so many dogs was finding a place to keep them. Betty finally arrived at what seemed like the perfect answer. She took her dogs out to an island in Quesnel Lake. Here they could run free and did not have to be tied. As well, the female dogs would not be bred by some Heinz 57-type of dog. This led to the island being named Virgin Island for a time, but finally the name was changed to Dog Island.

Since she didn't have any other place to put them, she schemed and plotted and finally came up with a brilliant idea. She asked for a grazing licence on the island. She had horses at the time, so it was only natural for Forestry to assume the licence was for her horses. When Betty went to pick up the licence the clerk said, "We forgot to fill in what the permit is for, but of course it is for the horses, isn't it?" When Betty announced that it was for her dogs, the ranger shouted, "No bloody way!" The idea didn't fly, but Betty sure got a laugh out of it. As she was walking out of the Forestry office she heard the ranger say, "That woman is insane!"

It was obvious that Forestry underestimated Betty because she had no intention of giving up. Her next mode of attack was to stake the island. She then applied for and got mineral claims. Since a part of the claim stretched onto the mainland, this gave her a place to build a cabin. The downside to the cabin was that when the dogs spotted people working on it, they swam over from the island. What to do? Betty thought it out and strung a boom around a portion of the island. When the dogs climbed over the boom she strung an electric fence on top of the boom logs. Along came a big wind and blew the logs on shore. She retaliated by driving nails into the logs, but the dogs climbed over them and got injured. It was a long drawn-out fight, and Betty finally gave up the island and found other accommodations for her dogs.

One thing Betty learned was just how easy it is to transform a good bear dog into a poor bear dog. In her case, one of her dogs got too close

Getting ready to ride to Bart Lake Camp for a moose and caribou hunt.

to a bear and received a slap. The result was a dog that refused to go near bears. The power in a bear's slap is formidable, as even large bull moose have learned the hard way.

Betty started her guide training in 1965 under Alfred Bowe at his ranch. In time she went on to sell food and even booze at the ranch. It seems apparent that she did whatever she had to do to earn a living. Five years as a schoolteacher added another chapter to her life.

Betty really hit her stride when she bought a trapline. This was the sort of life she loved and it fit in very well with her love of dogs. But things reached their peak when she bought her first guiding territory. From then on it was just one adventure after another.

Knowing of my intense interest in grizzly bears, Betty told me of several experiences with them. Although she never felt that she had been in a position of danger with bears, she had some surprises and a few thrills as well.

One bright sunny day when she was alone at her lodge on Quesnel Lake, she went outside to sunbathe in the nude. Suddenly she noticed two grizzly bears between her and the door of the lodge. She managed to get around to the other door and went inside to grab her rifle. When she got back to the front door, the bears were standing up with their paws on the seat of her quad, looking it over with great interest. She pointed her

Suntanning on top of the Land Rover.

rifle up in the air and fired a shot, and the bears scooted for cover. When she checked the quad where they had been standing, she found they had managed to put their claws right through the seat.

When Betty finished her story, she allowed that no real harm had been done but added that it could have ended up in a worse way. I couldn't resist the temptation so I said, "Yes, Betty, if people had found your dead, naked body with grizzly bear sign all around it, just try to imagine the rumours that could have floated around the Cariboo Region for a time."

Betty worked for the Keg in Williams Lake on Friday and Saturday nights and then headed for the trapline where she spent the rest of the week. She also put a lot of time into cutting and selling shakes to a man from Alberta, but since she could not get a permit to cut the shakes, much of it was done under cover of darkness. One way or another, she found a way to survive.

When I queried Betty about some of her trapping experiences she brightened up as a special memory returned. She and friends Joan and Paul were nearing her second cabin when they came to a set where an animal had broken loose with the trap in tow. Betty assumed it was a lynx and started following the tracks in the snow while her friends went to her cabin. She quickly determined that the animal was a wolverine because it kept going and didn't stop like a lynx would have. After a long chase and a drop of about 300 metres (1,000 feet), Betty arrived at Long Creek, a tributary that descends into Quesnel Lake, where she spotted the wolverine in the creek, hiding behind a large boulder. Betty had her .308 rifle along but she did not want to shoot it for fear of ruining the hide of what was obviously an exceptionally large wolverine. She moved around to get into a position where she could strike the animal on the head with the rifle butt and render it unconscious. She climbed onto the boulder so she could bring the butt of the rifle down on its head, but the water exploded and the wolverine lunged up and grabbed the butt of the rifle with its front legs. As Betty fell over backwards, the gun hit the rock and knocked the wolverine off into the deepest part of the creek. Since she had no other means at her disposal, she shot it with the rifle and damaged the fur value considerably.

Now the real fun began. Since it was about -25°C (-10°F), the animal started freezing fast. Betty left it lying on the snow and then hiked back up to the cabin, arriving at nine at night, where she related the events

The Cache Cabin on the trapline on the North Arm of Quesnel Lake.

to the others. Paul took his packsack and went to retrieve the wolverine, arriving back at the cabin at two in the morning.

When he got back to the cabin, Paul started having chest pains and was afraid he was having a heart attack. Early the next morning Betty instructed the other two to head down the mountain to the boat, which was tethered on the lakeshore. They took the sleeping bags and the wolverine hide with them. The temperature was rapidly dropping, so Betty set out to spring the rest of the traps and close the line for the winter. They had to get out of the area before the lake froze over. It didn't take long before she was in snow so deep that she had to give up and return to the cabin. By this time it was too late to make it down the mountain before dark.

What an interesting night she spent alone at that cabin. All she had to keep warm was a foil blanket and insulated underwear. Because of that she spent the long night trying to keep a fire going in her makeshift stove. As it turned out, it was a bright, cold, moonlit night. Sometime in the wee hours Betty happened to glance out the one and only window to behold an amazing sight: a small herd of caribou, silhouetted against the surrounding trees, and all standing motionless. Betty stayed as quiet as possible and eventually a few of the animals came and pressed their lips against the window, then stared into the cabin trying to understand what they were confronted with. Just another strange experience in Betty's many years of bush life.

Another wolverine she caught also led her on a merry chase. All she had with her for a weapon was a hammer and it took some time before she managed to strike it a good blow and render it senseless. Next, she had to make certain it was dead. Betty was at a loss about what to do until she remembered a technique used by trappers in the past. She stood on top of the wolverine's chest with her full weight directly over its heart. Compression did the trick, and the next time she checked the heart was still.

Betty recalled the time she and a hunter came along a ridge and walked into a herd of caribou. Then right before their eyes they saw a wolverine feeding on a caribou calf, which was already half-eaten. The herd immediately took off, having either scented or spotted them. The wolverine also disappeared at top speed, leaving them at a loss to understand why the herd seemed to show no fear of the wolverine in their midst.

Perhaps this can be better understood when we watch videos of the reactions of gnus, or wildebeests, after one of the herd is taken down by lions. Often the herd will stop running and return to feeding, totally ignoring the nearby lions as they enjoy their feast.

Betty and I discussed the days when guides were allowed to take their hunters in and fly the game back out by helicopters. Regrettably, this freedom was stopped because some people abused it terribly. I knew of one incident when a forest ranger took a helicopter into the mountains and returned two hours later with a caribou and a mountain goat slung beneath the chopper. A close look at the goat showed it had been shot from above, right in the top of its head. To add insult to injury, the taxpayers paid for that hunt.

It should not be hard to understand why I was one of many people who pleaded with the game officials to stop this type of slaughter, where animals had no possibility of escape. Only after the fact did I learn

Betty and a hunter with a young bull caribou at the lick on Long Creek.

that one helicopter pilot had seven caribou in Prince George at one time for shipment to Vancouver. All had been taken above timberline with a helicopter. The poor creatures had absolutely no chance of escape. I like to believe that all true sportsmen feel that animals deserve some sort of a chance. What kind of challenge is it to shoot an animal from a helicopter after it has been run to the point of total exhaustion?

Perhaps one of Betty's scariest moments came when she took a friend along on a trip around her trapline. In the process they had to follow along Quesnel Lake. Both had a dog team, a total of about a dozen dogs. As they followed the contour of the lake, they suddenly broke through the ice. Betty's feet touched bottom in about 1 metre (3 feet) of water, and then all hell broke loose. With no other option, Betty started breaking ice toward shore until she got into shallow water, where she managed to climb to the bank. The other trapper anchored his dog sled to the ice and came around to assist her. One by one they managed to get her dogs out on shore and then released the other team and they, in turn, all made it to safety.

At this point the worst was far from over as they were wet and losing body heat at a rapid rate. Just a short distance from that spot was a summer home, and Betty felt sure that a warm cabin awaited them. But when

Betty with two hunters from Colorado looking for caribou on Mount Steveson.

they arrived they found that the occupant had experienced a bout of cabin fever and had left for the winter. By no easy means they managed to get a fire started and, in turn, coaxed all 12 dogs inside where they could dry off and have a chance at survival. As for themselves, they had to hang their clothes to dry, and all they found in the cabin were two dirty pairs of wool underwear with the opening hatches on the back. They didn't smell very good but at least they managed to keep warm. That night they fretted about having to cross the same spot the next day, but a bit of good luck came their way when it turned cold. By morning they had a fresh sheet of safe ice to cross on their return home.

When the humane Conibear traps came into use, any trapper making $10,000 over a winter was given a $500 grant toward exchanging their traps for Conibears. Betty felt a twinge of pride when she managed to reach that target. What did it for her were martens, many of which brought in over $100 that winter.

Some people may remember the movie, *Nikki Wild Dog of the North*, which was filmed in Alberta. Betty had a chance to sell one of her prize dogs to the producers for $500. As a bonus, they were to give her two wolves after the movie was completed, on the condition that she would not give or sell them to anyone else. At the last minute her dog got sick and died, which of course killed the deal. But to Betty's surprise the two wolves were given to her anyway, and it turned out that she got great enjoyment from them.

Another rather exciting memory that concerned one of these wolves happened at her lodge. The wolf was tied up outside, not far from where she had fed some meat scraps to her dogs. That night there happened to be a full moon, and luckily so, for all at once she heard the dogs barking. She rushed to the door and looked out to behold the wolf and the horses both staring in the same direction. She grabbed her .30-30 and rushed out the door to see what was happening. As she got near the wolf, a big grizzly, obviously attracted by the meat, rose up out of the shadows. Betty fired the rifle and instantly the bear whirled and tumbled down the bank into the Cariboo River adjacent to the lodge. In the subdued light, she was certain she saw it drifting down the river so she gave up and went back into the lodge. The next day she followed the river for quite a distance but no trace of the bear was ever found.

Betty's guests at the Double T never went home without a healthy dose of adventure and charm.

There is one thing certain about spending years in the woods: sooner or later one is bound to get in a bind. The best we can do is use common sense and plan ahead as much as possible. More than one wise trapper has been saved from an icy death because of a good supply of firewood at all—and I repeat, all—of their cabins, without which they surely would have perished because of injury or prolonged sickness. If there is one exceptionally good piece of knowledge that should be given to people who spend lots of time in the woods during winter, it's how to build a snow cave. If one is sick or injured in sub-zero temperatures it is imperative to get to shelter or beneath the snow. And it follows that whatever action a person takes must be taken before hypothermia—with its resulting state of confusion—sets in.

The sun may be starting to set on Betty's endless wilderness adventures, but it appears obvious that her bush trails led her through a contented and successful life. As well, she has enough memories to last her for a thousand years.

4.

CANOEING THE RIVERS

A mong my memories is a story about the Fraser River. It concerns barrel racing, which happened for a few years back in the 1940s when I was just a lad. The races started at the Dome Creek Railway Bridge and ended at the Prince George Railway Bridge, a total distance of 232 kilometres (145 miles). They were sponsored by the Prince George Rotary Club, and the person guessing the closest to the time of travel was awarded a prize of $300, several months' pay at that time. The second prize was $100, and finally four prizes of $25. On the first race, trapper and guide J.B. Hooker of Dome Creek followed the barrel as far as the Grand Canyon where pioneer riverman George Williams took over for the remaining distance to Prince George. Taken along as witnesses were I.B. Guest and other Rotarians, whose mission was to keep the red-and-white barrel out of eddies and backwaters that would have impeded its travel and consequently delayed the barrel for who knows how long. In anticipation of the race one old-timer noted, "If it's 145 miles overall and the river runs at 5 miles an hour, and I allow for delay in the pool below the canyon, and a wind, as well as the odd back eddy, then the barrel should float in here in 52 hours, 1 minute and 45 seconds." That guess turned out to be remarkably close to the actual time.

The first barrel was launched at Dome Creek at 3 a.m. on July 3, 1943, and made it safely past the Hansard Bridge before disappearing during the hours of darkness. Confusion prevailed until it was found jammed under a fir log in the booming grounds at Sinclair Mills. This rendered the first race null and void, so the Rotary Club held an emergency meeting where it was ordered that a second barrel be launched from the Dome

Creek Bridge at 3 a.m. on July 10. This time a light was attached to the barrel to allow the crew to find and follow it in the dark. As well, a few inches of cement was placed in the barrel to keep the light on top of the barrel from being submerged. By the time the barrel reached Shelley the light had

Displaying life preservers. Photo Donn Moffat.

gone out, but the resourceful rivermen attached two flashlights and the show hit the road again. Several times the men had to row the boat to keep pace with the barrel. This was explained by the west wind taking a greater hold on the boat than on the partly submerged barrel.

When the barrel arrived at the finish line the total time was half a minute under 48 hours. Once again confusion arose because six contestants had guessed exactly 48 hours. This forced the Rotary Club to change the prize allotment. Perhaps some justice took place when Earl Jaeck of Penny was one of the winners, as he had been gracious enough to deliver coffee and doughnuts to the rivermen accompanying the barrel when they reached Penny. The first-place prize of $300 was divided into six prizes of $50 each, and the second-place prize of $100 was won by Mrs. H. Withiam, whose husband spent years showing movies along the railway line east of Prince George during the 1940s and '50s.

At 10 p.m. on June 24, 1944, another red-and-white barrel left the Dome Creek Bridge. The proceeds from both years' events were to go toward a playground for children in Prince George. Once again J.B. Hooker was in charge of the accompanying boat.

The travel time of the barrel was 55 hours, 45 minutes and 13.6 seconds. Just how they managed to get the 0.6 of a second was not explained. Because of the six-person tie the previous year, contestants were urged to add minutes and seconds to their guesses, and thankfully they did. The $300 prize winner was A. Champayne with a time of 55 hours, 45 minutes and 12 seconds. The next closest was Earl Messmer with a

Along the Nechako. Photo Donn Moffat.

time of 55 hours, 45 minutes and 10 seconds. Take note that the race took place in the high water of June. This means that the current travelled just under 5 kilometres (3 miles) per hour on average. This is a far cry from the 16 to 24 kilometres (10 to 15 miles) per hour that some folks claim the river travels.

The river log noted:

Thursday 10 p.m.—Barrel launched promptly on the hour and immediately came under convoy of powered riverboat piloted by J.B. Hooker and carrying I.B. Guest. Hot night, no-see-ums and mosquitoes in swarms.

Friday 3:20 a.m.—At Slim Creek. So cold no flies or mosquitoes around. Barrel travelling slow—slower than last year when river was higher.

6 a.m.—Stopped at Jaeck's mill for coffee and phoned Prince George. Up to this point two hours behind last year. Strong headwind and heavy rain.

1 p.m.—Passing A.E.C. Reid's at Longworth. Sunny out and quite comfortable. Should be at head of Grand

Canyon about 3:45 p.m. Strong headwind and rain continuing. Thunder. Fear boat might tip.

4:50 p.m.—Shot through canyon and ten minutes later through lower canyon with J.B. Hooker proving himself a real expert as a river boatman. Waited for barrel that took 30 minutes to come through lower canyon while sun shone warmly.

Saturday 3 a.m.—Passed Hansard Bridge.

5 a.m.—At 104 mile [Upper Fraser]. Clear and frosty. Water at this point slow, wide and sluggish. Ran ahead three miles to build fire, warm ourselves and have breakfast.

8 a.m.—Barrel not moving more than two miles an hour. Cold wind continues.

4:20 p.m.—Stopped at McLean's Camp six miles above Giscome Portage and Mrs. Mitchell's farm. Still blowing and showering.

9:30 p.m.—Passing Willow River; still bucking strong headwind.

Sunday 12:15 a.m.—Met A.B. Moffat and Bill Ranby at McLean's Sawmill, at Shelley. They came out by car to determine the needs of the crew. Boat continued to convoy barrel till daylight, while rain poured down.

4:15 a.m.—Light on barrel continuing to show up well. Passing John Porter's place. Ran ahead of barrel and waited at steel bridge at Prince George.

The 1945 version of the barrel race was joined by *Citizen* staff writer Clem Russell. He and famous river-hog George Williams along with

Harold Assman were joined by guide J.B. Hooker at Dome Creek. They dropped the barrel off at the bridge at 10 p.m. and then set off by riverboat. Some of Russell's notes were as follows:

> We slipped by Slim Creek at 2:55 a.m. We were 25 minutes ahead of last year's time and we gained a further 15 minutes by Penny, reached Longworth at 11:30 a.m. and dawdled by Hungry Creek toward the upper canyon as headwinds built up. Ashore above the canyon, we quickly boiled coffee, wolfed sandwiches, and then saw the barrel enter the upper reaches at 3:45 p.m., giving it a few minutes lead while we lashed down our duffle.
>
> We sped past the rock where four friends of George Williams perished in construction days, grazed by the whirlpools which had claimed their toll of lives in early days, glided over the pond-like middle reaches and bounced into the lower canyon past a whirlpool which had sucked down a barge and its crew to add to the 100 lives or so that the Fraser claimed in one season.
>
> While we shot 20 minutes downstream, then returned in search of the barrel, both Jim and George related pages of the early history of settlement, when steamboats plied out of Tête Jaune [Cache], their skippers in bitter rivalry with bargemen. It was an almost forgotten phase of the pioneer spirit which built the north, leaving behind ghost towns and camps, once boisterous in their heyday. On a sandbar we unloaded the boat, preparatory to the two veterans re-entering the canyon to search for the barrel, when we had the best laugh of the trip.
>
> A family of raucous Canadian jays convoyed the barrel into sight, the adult birds fiercely struggling toward it against the current before it disdained their clamor and slid around a rock island out of the canyon at 4:45 p.m.
>
> Tales of fact or fancy, told with the easy familiarity of men who had known many a lonely campfire, and whose veracity it would have been discourteous to question, whiled away the hours as we drifted to Sinclair Mills,

reached at 8:10 p.m. Hundreds of swallows swooped and tilted in mid-air out of picturesque clay nests under the eaves of mill buildings, decimating skeeters quicker than we could swat the pests which caused our first discomfort between there and Dewey.

It was along this stretch that a swirl of water like the boils we had passed below rapids caught our eye, in time to see the head of a sturgeon on its way upriver. The giant startled us. A cow and calf moose above the McGregor River at 5:50 a.m. prompted us to paddle across river to try snapshots of the sublime ugliness of the little fellow, then we again hit headwinds and loafed past King Oscar's mine toward Giscome Rapids where George Williams spent 15 years as helmsman, taking the run in two stages. Giscome Portage offered a glance at the famed clay deposits ...

This barrel arrived at the Prince George Bridge in a time of 52 hours, 35 minutes and 35 seconds. D.A. McFarlane of Hutton won first prize with a guess of 5 seconds less than the actual time. This was the last barrel run and many people agreed that Prince George had lost an inspirational and romantic part of its history with the closure. But life goes on, and as we shall see, other challenges took off where the barrel run ended.

THE CANOE CHALLENGES

There were many canoe races of note, and one that deserves recognition was the Bowron Lakes Wilderness Canoe Races. The race held in 1970 was won by noted canoeists Steve Schwartz and Costo Bush, both of Prince George. Their total time was 14 hours and 52 minutes for the 118-kilometre (72-mile) distance with its portages.

NORTHWEST BRIGADE CANOE RACE

Some adventures start out as an inspiration and then turn into an institution. Such was the case with the canoe race that started at Fort St. James and followed the Nechako River to Prince George. Originally started by Bill Blackburn and Chris Switzer of Prince George in 1958,

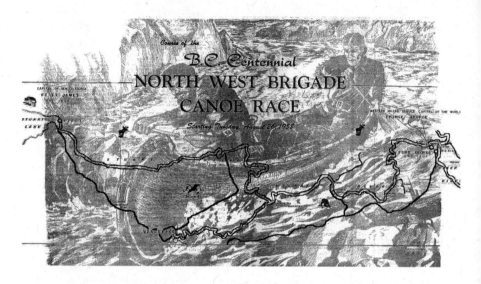

Map of Northwest Brigade Canoe Race. Courtesy Bill Blackburn.

it ran until 1967 and eventually turned into an event dominated by top-notch canoeists.

There is a rather rough canyon on the Stuart River shortly after it leaves Stuart Lake, dependent on the height of the river; there are also several sets of rapids along the Stuart and Nechako rivers. All told this turned out to be a tiring trip of 240 kilometres (146 miles), as it is 92 kilometres (56 miles) from the mouth of the Stuart to Prince George. Because of the nature of this trip, it soon attracted the top canoeists from across Canada as well as from the US.

Several of the winners of these races were world-class canoeists and took part in the centennial cross-Canada race from Rocky Mountain House, Alberta, to Expo '67 in Montreal (see Chapter 5, Les Voyageurs). The champions of the 10 years of these races are as follows:

1958 – Frank Buchanon and Jim Miller
1959 – Ralph Sawyer and Gerry Wagner
1960 – Bob Buchanon and Herbe Brade
1961 – Bob Buchanon and Herbe Brade
1962 – Herbe and Art Brade
1963 – Costo Bush and Dave Hentges
1964 – Gib McEachern and Norm Crerar
1965 – Gib McEachern and Norm Crerar

1966 – Dave Hentges and Roy Jackson
1967 – Gene Scott and Jim Robertson

Of special interest to me was that Gib McEachern and Norm Crerar were two of the top canoeists on the Manitoba team that won the Fort St. James to Victoria race in 1966 and the 5,282-kilometre (3,283-mile) centennial race to Expo in 1967. This demonstrates that the Fort St. James races were frequented by many of the top canoeists in the game, some of whom came from Minnesota, a canoeing paradise.

THE NORTHERN HARDWARE CANOE RACE

The canoe race from Isle de Pierre to Prince George began in 1960 and became an annual event until 1984. It was sponsored by the Northern Hardware Store in Prince George and overseen by Donn Moffat. Known as the Northern Hardware Canoe Race, it wasn't long before it became a much-anticipated event for many Prince George area residents. In due course it attracted over 70 notable canoeists annually from far and wide.

Fighting Nechako rapids. Photo Donn Moffat.

One of Donn's more memorable events took place in White Mud Rapids on the Nechako River. One of the noted canoeists, Costo Bush, was reluctant to wear a floatation device—called a life jacket at that time— which was stipulated in the race format. In desperation, Donn told him to put it on around his waist if it chafed him too much. No sooner had the race started at Isle de Pierre than Costo took off his floatation device and threw it into the canoe. A short time later they entered the White Mud Rapids where the canoe was flipped downside up. Costo, a non-swimmer, was fighting for his life when one of the half-dozen safety boats came to his rescue. In future races Costo faithfully wore his floatation device.

Northern Hardware Canoe Race. Photo Donn Moffat.

Throughout the 25 years of the May 24 race from Isle de Pierre to the Hudson's Bay Slough in Prince George, the times differed considerably due to the height and speed of the river. A headwind or a tailwind made a big difference in the times taken to run the 64-kilometre (40-mile) course. Novices were allowed in the race and were given the advantage of a 15-minute head start.

Ron Williams of Smithers won three firsts in a row, from 1976 to 1979, plus two more in 1983–84. But Ron went one better. In 1980 he and partner Serge Corbin of Cap-de-la-Madeleine, Quebec, whom many considered the best paddler in the world, won the world championship canoe marathon and the International Classic race in Quebec, the world's most prestigious canoe race. As if that wasn't enough, they went on to win the 1981 Hyack Canoe Race from Hope to New Westminster, and followed that up the next day by winning the Northern Hardware race. Gracious in victory, Ron acknowledged that the second-place winners, Tom Blackburn and Harry James, "would place in the top ten at the world championships." Tom and Harry fought neck and neck down the course—often talking to the champs to pass the time—only to lose at the end of the race. Ron Williams had a different partner for the next race in 1982; they didn't win but came in only one second behind the winners.

This in spite of the fact that Williams had won his third straight Hyack race the previous day. All things considered, it appears that the 42-year-old Williams must have been among the best canoeists in the game.

Herbe Brade also won first three times in a row, from 1961 to 1963. As well, he had six first-place wins for the all-time record in the Northern Hardware Canoe Race.

Following are the winners of the adult race throughout its 25-year existence.

1960 Bob and Frank Buchanon — 3 hours, 50 minutes.
1961 Herbe Brade and Bob Buchanon — 3 hours, 57 minutes.
1962 Herbe Brade and Gerald Ploughman — 4 hours, 15 minutes.
1963 Herbe Brade and Cliff Auger —3 hours, 52 minutes.
1964 Bernie Gauthier and Costo Bush — 3 hours, 50 minutes.
1965 Adolf Teufele and Roy Jackson — 3 hours, 48 minutes.
1966 Herbe Brade and Dick Hart — 3 hours, 15 minutes.
1967 Gene Scott and Jim Robertson — 3 hours, 42 minutes.
1968 Dick Hart and Roy Jackson — 3 hours, 57 minutes.
1969 Costo Bush and Harry Schwartz — 4 hours, 23 minutes.
1970 Dave Hentges and Herbe Brade — 4 hours, 16 minutes.
1971 Dave Hentges and Herbe Brade — 3 hours, 58 minutes.
1972 Sven Davidson and Bernie Gauthier — 3 hours, 45 minutes.
1973 Merl Gordon and Bruce Hawkenson — 4 hours, 5 minutes.
1974 Merl Gordon and Bruce Hawkenson — 3 hours, 52 minutes.
1975 John Lee and Dennis Wick — 4 hours, 29 minutes.
1976 Bruce Hawkenson and Ron Williams — 3 hours, 51 minutes.
1977 Bruce Hawkenson and Ron Williams — 3 hours, 55 minutes.
1978 John Buckley and Ron Williams — 4 hours, 12 minutes.
1979 Paul Sollens and Shaun McAdams— 3 hours, 54 minutes.
1980 Harry James and Steve Schwartz — 4 hours, 35 minutes.
1981 Serge Corbin and Ron Williams — 4 hours, 9 minutes.
1982 Harry James and Tom Blackburn — 4 hours, 1 minute.
1983 Al Rudquist and Ron Williams — 4 hours, 14 minutes.
1984 Al Rudquist and Ron Williams — 4 hours, 3 minutes.

The fastest time was 3 hours and 15 minutes, which probably indicates high water levels and consequently a faster current.

Winner Ron Williams (on right). Photo Don Moffat.

Were there any surprises during those years? How about the 1982 race just mentioned. Imagine paddling for 64 kilometres and losing the $800 prize by just one second. Something else that appears obvious is that the costs of sponsoring the race kept growing as the years passed. When the races finally ended in 1984 the prizes had grown to $5,000. As to fatalities, there were none in all the years of racing down the Nechako River. The Ploughman brothers drowned while training in Summit Lake, but that does not indicate that they were novices; Gerald Ploughman, with his partner Herbe Brade, won first prize in 1962.

To give an idea of how widespread an area the entrants came from, let's look at the 20th Northern Hardware race in 1979. Two canoeists from Montana, Shaun McAdams and Paul Sollens had run the 137-kilometre (83-mile) Hyack Canoe Race from Hope to New Westminster where they came in third. Immediately after that race the two men drove all night to get to Isle de Pierre in time for the Northern Hardware race, which they won. The winners of the Hyack race, Ron Williams of Smithers and Luke Robillard of Vermont had also driven all night and finished third in the Northern Hardware race. This shows that many of the 37 entrants were world-class canoeists who followed the racing circuit and often paddled at 60 strokes per minute. Just what it took to win was demonstrated by Steve Schwartz of Prince George. He had been running the race for 16 years and finally won it in 1980 with co-pilot Harry James. It was noted that the winners kept up a steady 69 strokes per minute, indicating the gruelling training regimen they followed.

Northern Hardware put a great amount of finances and effort into these races; the planning alone required a lot of time. Along with all the prize money, three canoes were given away in draws. After the races were over it was party time, and the records indicate that a pretty penny was spent on beer. I also noticed in among Donn Moffat's notes that Bob Harkins was badly needed to get the message out to the people. Soon that request was answered and Bob was along in the CKPG boat, doing live broadcasts as the racers made their way downriver. Donn's notes indicated that the races received a helpful lift when Bob Harkins started travelling with the boats. It made a profound difference and added colour to the events.

When I asked Donn if there had been any attempt at cheating, he replied, "There were rules about the canoes, they had to be 18 feet long [5.5 metres], but some entrants did try and cheat a little by modifying

Bob Buchanon and Bob Harkins in the CKPG boat.

the bottom a little to gain speed. Finally we had to get some referees, such as Bill Blackburn, to keep the race fair to all."

The race was divided into three classes: professionals, seniors and novices. Something that added a lot of interest and got parents involved was that anyone under the age of 19 had to have their parents sign for them. Some of the entrants' names leap out from the lists, such as Kevin Moffat, who came in first in the novices' race of 1975, and Pat Glazier, who came in third in the same race.

Safety boats were always on the job and sometimes they were certainly needed, such as in the 1974 race when seniors Roland Chartrand and Dennis Downey rolled in the White Mud Rapids for the record third time. Chartrand explained, "All of a sudden we just saw pieces of cedar flying by; it's hard to say what happened, the rollers were just too big. That's the worst that I've been in!"

⸎

When Northern Hardware dropped the canoe races on the Nechako, it was by no means the end of canoeing along the river. People still enjoy its flood-controlled waters. On July 3, 1992, Maxine and Peter Koppe, who live along the banks of the Nechako River, left Takla Landing in their canoe. Their destination was Prince George about 360 kilometres (220 miles) distant. During the trip Maxine faithfully recorded their experiences in a journal that she graciously loaned to me. I have just taken some of the highlights from their trip, all the while wishing I could have gone along.

DAY 1 — No sooner had they started paddling down Takla Lake (down meaning toward the outlet) than a wind arose and whitecaps appeared in droves. They carried on for about another 30 minutes before they took a break; then they paddled for another hour with the wind steadily increasing. It wasn't long until they were taking water over the sides of their canoe; this forced them to make camp. Judging by the strange action of their canoe, they suspected that it was loaded front heavy. They planned to make corrections before the next day's travel.

DAY 2 — They awoke to a clear sky with a calm lake, so they crossed at the narrowest spot; this gave them access to the many appealing beaches that always seem to be on the opposite side of the lake. The changes they made in the load placement appeared to work, and so they were well on their way. As they silently paddled along the lake, a mama duck appeared carrying all her ducklings on her back. Maxine noted that she had never seen that before. Eventually they stopped at a beautiful creek and "caught a fish every cast," according to Maxine. They estimated that they had already covered half the distance along Takla Lake.

DAY 3 — The plan to do a bit of sailing was put to action as soon as they got out on the lake at 9:30. It immediately became apparent that although it was easier than paddling, it was also slower. In time they arrived at a Forestry campsite, which was accessible by road. Since there were campers on site, they decided to be unsociable and left for more private settings.

Does a hard day of paddling allow a full night's sleep? It could have, but as it turned out they hit the sack for an interrupted sleep. During the night an animal hung around for a while and even bumped into the tent a few times. At last they resorted to some shrill whistling, which drove it away and allowed them a bit of sleep.

The rising sun warming their tent brought them back to the land of the living. Back on the water, the paddlers were treated to the cries of a loon. Maxine noted how wonderful it sounded and added something that few would disagree with: "A lake just doesn't seem right without loons."

DAY 4 — This started out badly with high winds that kept them off the lake until well into the afternoon. Naturally this caused a bit of restlessness to set in, so they tried a test run with the empty canoe. It went well so they broke camp and were just getting ready to leave when a cub bear walked near their tent. They didn't see mama bear but felt glad to be getting out of there anyway. They put up the sail and were drifting along when a loon surfaced right beside their canoe, causing surprises all around.

Maxine and Peter Koppe.

DAY 5 — After several hours on the water they stopped for a rest at

Martin Graingier's cabins where Peter caught a big dolly (bull trout), which provided them with their main meal of the day. As they stood around relaxing, their world suddenly erupted into an ear-splitting racket as a cottonwood tree came crashing down just upstream of them. Water sprayed in all directions, and when things settled down they realized that a beaver had just finished his logging contract.

DAY 6 — Our adventurers were up and out on the lake early, so after three hours of paddling they arrived at Trembleur Lake. They were thoroughly enjoying the beautiful weather, so they stopped on a beach and soaked up some sun. No sooner did they get underway again than the wind picked up. Their goal had been to cover the 3 kilometres (2 miles) to the narrowest part of the lake, which they intended to cross early the next morning before the wind picked up. Their hope to make camp was frustrated because there was garbage strewn all along the lakeshore, so they had to keep paddling against a powerful headwind. When the lake got even wilder, they gave up and found a decent campsite off the lake a ways. After the camp was set up and dinner had been served, they paddled to where some beavers had a logging show underway. Huge cottonwood trees were down and three beavers spotted, each of whom showed their displeasure to the intruders. In the middle of the night the beavers got their revenge—they swam right beside the tent and slapped their tails on the water; this went on for at least an hour, or as Maxine put it, "Long enough for me to contemplate how beaver steaks would taste for breakfast."

That afternoon they found a large bull moose with a massive set of antlers that had drifted in against the shore of the lake. As it still had its antlers, it was obvious that it had broken through the ice in early winter. The cold water had preserved it quite well.

DAY 7 — Up at five and on the lake by 6:30. They crossed the lake as planned to avoid the extra paddling it would have taken had they followed the shoreline. They were now about 16 kilometres (10 miles) from the Tachie River. Maxine caught a big rainbow, which they decided to keep. Then, as luck would have it, Peter caught another which was hooked so badly they had to keep it. That made it a given what the evening meal would consist of.

Just short of the Tachie River they stopped and ate lunch on a scenic rock bluff overlooking the lake. While Peter soaked up some sun, Maxine indulged in some red-hot fishing; then it was down the Tachie River to face the first rapids of their journey. The river was a bit of a disappointment with its slow current, swampy banks and endless willows along the shores.

Once past the Grand Rapids Indian Reserve they scouted the first rapids, which was not easy with all the thick underbrush along the banks. They ran the rapids on river left without a problem, except for a lot of boils that tended to throw the canoe around a lot. When they arrived at the second set of rapids, they scouted both and breezed through without a sweat. Then it was quiet water right through to Stuart Lake.

Fighting a continuous headwind all day, they spent 11 hours at the paddles with more to go before a decent camping spot was found. This was the only time Maxine expressed disappointment with the trip: garbage, plastic of all colours and sizes, dirty diapers and old shoes were strewn along the lakeshore for miles.

DAY 8 — Awakened at 7 a.m. by a large animal walking beside the tent. Peter hollered a few times and it left; they assumed it was a moose or bear. Out on the water Maxine gleefully noted the beaches that went on forever. To pass the time they started beachcombing and shortly wound up with one basketball, one orange ball, two paddles and an orange-coloured plastic sled. For a change of pace, Peter paddled the canoe near shore while Maxine experienced how nice it was to get out and walk. By early afternoon they arrived at a friend's cabin at Pinchi Bay and spent the rest of the day doing laundry and resting up.

DAY 9 — Spent some time paddling close to shore and picked out 15 First Nations pictographs along the rock bluffs facing the lake. There were portions of several more that had broken off or washed away. They had a most interesting lunch break by stopping on a point across from Honeymoon Island. After 20 minutes of enjoying the view, a couple came along on Sea-Doos and they also decided it was a good spot to have lunch. They left and shortly returned with their houseboat, kids, dogs, etc. The dogs seemed to be the nicest part of the group so it was back into the canoe and on to another camping spot.

As they neared Fort St. James they stopped to ask about the condition of the Stuart Canyon just a short distance down the Stuart River. As luck had it, they stopped at the wrong place and the people turned out to be friends who had just arrived 20 minutes earlier. This resulted in a nice respite along with a refreshing drink.

After replenishing a few supplies in Fort St. James, they headed downriver and stopped at a privately owned campground for the night. As they packed all their equipment up from the river, an elderly woman watched them with keen interest. Each time Maxine passed by, the woman asked a question, such as, "Have you had a long day?" Maxine nodded in the affirmative. Then she asked, "How far have you travelled?"

Maxine responded with, "Oh, about 200 kilometres."

This caused the woman to reply, "My heavens, you have had a long day."

Maxine didn't bother to explain, in part because she was too busy laughing.

The camp cost $10 for the night, but the shower alone was worth it and then some. In the evening they walked down and scouted out the Stuart Canyon, and then made a few phone calls to determine the state of the Chinlac Rapids farther downriver. The information they received made it sound pretty scary.

DAY 10 — They were off on the river before 10 a.m. and shot through the Stuart Canyon without difficulty. They ran it on river right, which in low water would be too shallow. Except for a few haystack waves, it was quite easy to run. After the dead water they had endured, it was a pleasure to find a bit of current with rather scenic shores, a definite improvement over the Middle and Tachie rivers.

Peter's 32-kilogram (70-pound) chinook salmon. Photo Peter Koppe.

They attempted to put up the sail, only to find the sail stem broken. It was then back to the paddles, which worked well because they had a tailwind for once. Just for a nice change, they drifted along for an hour or so and then stopped at an abandoned farm for a rest. It turned out to be the original home of author Olive Fredrickson, who wrote *Silence of the North*.

Back on the river, they paddled for a few more hours and then stopped at an abandoned farm to camp for the night. It looked as if someone was keeping cattle there but none were seen. No sooner did they get the tent set up than they heard an enormous amount of bawling and six young heifers came bounding up to them. They debated whether they should move on, but other camp spots were hard to find because they were passing through so much private land. They decided to stay. The heifers eventually left and ran across the creek Maxine and Peter were camped beside; then they began running around in circles, as though they were playing.

DAY 11 — Two canoeists got an early start this day because the six heifers returned with their parents, aunts, uncles and cousins. Maxine wrote that they felt quite insignificant when faced with such a monster herd. She also suggested that *America's Funniest Home Videos* would have had a sure winner if they had taped the show that followed. She was standing outside in her underwear waving a paddle and trying to scare away the herd of cows. They obliged by running a short way but then returned for round two. They were harder to scare the second time so it required both of them to man the paddles and do some exotic type of dance. Then two large bulls appeared and stared at them as if they were fresh from a nuthouse. Maxine swears she heard some of the cows snickering, but fortunately the young heifers broke ranks and ran off. The cows slowly followed and eventually the two bulls joined them. After they crossed the creek, they all stopped and stared back at these strange creatures that yelled and waved things. On the chance that the herd was regrouping for round three, Maxine and Peter broke camp and were on the river by 5 a.m.

Back on the water, it was just a short jaunt to Mandalay Ranch and then they were in a lot of rapids for about 25 kilometres (15 miles). The rapids were very fast but didn't require much manoeuvring. Finally at 10:30 they arrived at the most dangerous part of the rapids. They spent a lot of time scouting each set of rapids before running them, and found they were much less than what they had imagined them to be. The waves of the Chinlac Rapids were not the 2- to 3-metre (7- to 10-foot) waves they had been told about. They were less than 1 metre (3 feet) in height, but still impressive. For those who might wish to run these rapids, take note that Maxine and Peter ran all of these on extreme river right and stated that the lower section was the most impressive. They breezed through just as they had planned while scouting it, and were quite pleased with themselves, even though they did take some water over the sides.

A pleasant surprise awaited them as they spotted a cow moose in water up to her neck, eating the willows around her. As she spent lots of time underwater, they slowly paddled along when she wasn't looking. Their journal pointed out something that I had observed many times throughout the years: it is surprising how long moose can stay underwater without surfacing.

This is the beauty of canoeing, the ability to be one with nature, to be able to move in silence, hearing and seeing the wonders of the wild.

They continued paddling on down to the site of the Chinlac Indian Reserve, where the people were slaughtered by Chilcotin Natives long ago. It was a steep climb up from the river, but it was a nice place to camp so they packed everything up the hill. The Natives chose well in having their camp at this spot, as there is little snow or precipitation; as a result, it has totally different plant life than adjacent areas.

After a change of clothes, Maxine and Peter spent a bit of time looking for artifacts. None was found, but they were in for a surprise anyway. A lot of horse droppings led them to wonder why a horse would be in this deserted area. Then they came upon a spot where a horse had been tethered for some time and noticed a rope, mane, and horse's tail. A short distance away they came upon a horse's leg bone and hoof. At last they reasoned that a horse had wandered in wearing a halter and lead rope. It had spent some time feeding in the area until it got the rope tangled up in some brush. Unable to move, the poor creature slowly died from lack of food and water. These thoughts haunted the two canoeists throughout much of the night as they felt pity for that animal.

They also noted that bald eagles were in abundance along the rivers, probably waiting for the salmon runs to begin. An estimated 100 eagles had been spotted since their journey began. Out on the river they saw another cow moose; like the others they had seen, all three were dry cows. This begged some questions: "Where were all the bulls last fall?" and "Are there too many predators around this area?"

DAY 12 — They were awakened at 5:30 as a moose strolled by their tent, then it was back to sleep. When they finally got up it was to greet a perfect day, except for a cold wind. Maxine glanced around the clearing to behold a doe deer about 100 metres (330 feet) distant. Unaware of their presence, she put on a grand show. She was eating in some saskatoon bushes when a bee or hornet stung her. She bounced up in the air, turned and kicked the bushes several times. When she returned to her eating, she got stung again. This time she got serious with the bush, kicking with her hind feet and slashing with her front feet. She stayed about 20 minutes before she wandered away. Maxine followed her for another 10 minutes without the deer being aware of her presence.

Their lunch break was taken at the Isle de Pierre ferry, and then it was down to the rapids where, because of high water levels, the river was wild and fast. They scouted it just to be safe. The logjam below the island was almost completely covered with water, as was most of the island. The river below the rapids had some large waves and lots of boils. After scouting the rapids, they ran through on the left side of the river and it worked well. They decided to camp above the White Mud Rapids and run them in the morning, so they made camp on an island. After three days of fighting headwinds, the calm air was greatly appreciated.

DAY 13 — On the last day of their trip, they lazed around and finally got on the river at 10:30. Fifty minutes of paddling took them to the White Mud Rapids. They scouted the first rapid, which was unnecessary, as they ran it with ease on the left side of the river and then crossed to river right to attack the main rapid. It was impressive at this high-water level with 2-metre (7-foot) waves in the centre and a nasty-looking keeper nearby. There was also another keeper on the right side just above the main rapid. They pulled into an eddy, where they fished for a while, and then found old piles of firewood that had endured from the days of the sternwheelers. It seems hard to believe, but some of this fir wood is still sound after being piled there for over 90 years. From the rapids it was an easy paddle to Prince George, where the two canoeists felt a sense of sadness that their trip was over. At the same time, it was good to be home.

While I was reading Maxine's journal I promised I would add a thought when I got to the end. It refers to the tree falling near the canoeists. This sort of thing has caused people to wonder how a tree can fall when there is no wind. Surely it follows that the trees should fall when it is windy and they are under stress. If you experience a tree going down when it is perfectly still, it is probably caused by beavers.

⌣

Of all my memories of the woods, canoeing is among the most special ones. If there is anything on earth more peaceful than paddling along through the early-morning fog I am not aware of it. It is another world, where silence is the order of the day, where one can sneak up on a moose

Buck Buchanon on Summit Lake.
Photo Donn Moffat.

feeding on aquatic plants, sit motionless and watch it feed until it gets human scent and heads for cover. And always, the sounds of nature abound, such as the call of a loon as it echoes back from the surrounding ridges. This is the sort of thing that awaits those who canoe the backcountry. I like to believe that canoeing will never die, and thankfully it seems there are others who feel the same way.

Some people are not satisfied with doing things the normal way. Such a man was trader/ trapper Buck Buchanon, who demonstrated that it was possible to paddle around Summit Lake in a washtub. I had heard about this sort of thing when I was a youngster, but I always thought it was just a joke. Buck proved that it is indeed possible. What I wonder about is how does one prevent the tub from going in circles? From what I have heard and read, Buck was an exceptional individual who spent many years in the woods. One did not trap the Far North, as he did back in the 1930s, without the ability to make the difficult seem rather easy. Speaking for myself, I think I will stick to canoes. Somehow I can't picture Buck going through Hell's Gate canyon in his mode of travel.

5.

LES VOYAGEURS

As a prelude to the centennial cross-Canada canoe race of 1967, local canoe clubs vied for the right to represent British Columbia. The entrants were greatly inspired by the awareness that upon arriving at Expo, each winning crew member would receive $2,500, with second-place crew members getting $2,000 each, and third place, $1,500. All crew members who completed the race were to receive $1,000.

During June 1966 a joint Prince George/Kamloops team won time trials on the North Thompson River, making the 64-kilometre (40-mile) trip from Barriere to Kamloops in 4 hours and 17 minutes. All members of the team then went into a rigorous training regimen in preparation for the big races. Bill Blackburn of Prince George was elected commodore and said that he would be satisfied with a fourth-place finish against the stiff competition provided by the other provinces.

A select group of canoeists was chosen from each province, and they went into a dynamic training program. Included among the canoeists were lawyers, miners, farmers, guides, trappers, musicians, students, railroaders, Indian chiefs, Inuit hunters, schoolteachers and labourers, not to mention professional skiers and paddlers.

On June 22, 1966, the *Prince George Citizen* carried the following editorial:

> B.C. Centennial canoe Commodore Bill Blackburn deserves a tip of the topper for his work in guaranteeing that this province is represented in the 100th anniversary canoe races this year and next. Not only that but also Prince

George men will make up half the team that competes in the inter-provincial events.

The B.C. canoe will be paddled by a composite crew from this city and Kamloops. They won the right on the weekend in trials at Kamloops. The thing about the centennial cross-Canada race in 1967 and the dash downriver this summer is that without Mr. Blackburn's urging, cajoling and promotion, B.C. might not have been represented at all.

A canoe enthusiast, he saw it as most suitable for centennial participation, but, at first, there wasn't too much interest from others. It will be a different story now.

The voyageurs make an entirely appropriate theme for recollection of our historical association. Their competition against teams from the remainder of the country will be followed with keen interest by residents of the entire province, and, particularly, Prince George. It's a great sport, demanding top condition and dedication. The centennial races could well do much toward stimulating a re-awakened interest in canoeing as a competitive sport and as recreation. Bill Blackburn will deserve much of the credit in these parts for this development.

In preparation for the 5,282-kilometre (3,283-mile) race from Rocky Mountain House, Alberta, to Montreal, many shorter training races were held. In 1966 ten six-men crews raced from Fort St. James to Victoria in replicas of the Voyageur canoes, which played an important part in the history of Canada. Eight metres (26 feet) in length and double-pointed, they were specially adapted for running rapids and large lakes, and were capable of carrying a ton of cargo plus their crews. The downside to the canoes was that they were made of fibreglass and weighed over 45 kilograms (100 pounds) more than the original chestnut canoes. Eight provinces were represented, plus the Yukon and Northwest Territories. Newfoundland and Prince Edward Island did not participate.

The BC canoe was appropriately dubbed the *Simon Fraser*; its team captain, Roy Jackson of Kamloops, had earned his place by winning the Flin Flon Gold Rush canoe race in 1951. For a capper, he had also won the Banff to Calgary canoe race the previous summer. Team member Herb Sievers, a contractor from Kamloops, was a member of several kayak clubs in Europe prior to coming to Canada. Harry Schwartz, a Prince George logging contractor, as well as a part-time trapper and guide, was twice runner-up in the BC championships. Harvey Fraser, a Kamloops construction superintendent, had a four-year professional record and was on the provincial championship team the previous year. Prince George residents Costo Bush and Dave Hentges were on the 1962 provincial winning team. Herbe Brade, a Prince George faller, was Northwest Brigade champion the three previous years. Dick Hart, a Kamloops truck driver, was a winner in the previous year's final.

The August 6–15, 1966, canoe race from Fort St. James to Victoria was a major test for the men. The first prize of $1,000 was expected to pull a few more strokes per minute out of the crews. Six team members manned the canoes, with two spares changing off from day to day. After leaving Fort St. James, the crews had to face the Stuart Canyon and then several sets of rapids in the Nechako River. The first lap was won by BC with a 19-second lead over Manitoba, but the second lap was taken by Manitoba when its team paddled the 128 kilometres (80 miles) down the Nechako River to the Prince George Bridge in a time of 8 hours, 16 minutes and 45 seconds.

This map shows the route for the last segment of the race—New Westminster to Victoria.

Their arrival at the Prince George Bridge had Manitoba in the lead; this was a situation that would prevail throughout almost all of the races. BC did itself proud as it usually came in second and won many of the sprints that were carried out in communities along the way: Prince George, Quesnel, Hope, Mission, New Westminster, Kitsilano, Galiano Island, Sidney and Victoria.

The third leg of the trials presented difficulties when the racers ran into a great number of logs in Cottonwood Canyon. The Manitoba canoe managed to contact one of the logs, but serious problems were avoided and a warm welcome awaited the canoeists at Quesnel, where thousands turned out to greet the Voyageurs with their colourful headbands, sashes and bright shirts. A sprint was held from Hidden Paradise to Quesnel, with Manitoba winning.

As an aside, Hidden Paradise was located 4 kilometres (6 miles) upriver of Quesnel. It was a place of beauty owned by Jimmy and Georgie Donnelly. They built several cabins that they let for free to people who were hard done by during World War II. Brightly coloured pheasants strode amid myriad flowers including 200 varieties of roses. This lent an aura of wonder to one of the most spectacular spots in the entire Cariboo region. The Donnellys sold out in 1969.

The *Citizen* wrote:

> Thousands of cheering, shouting Quesnel residents turned out Monday night to welcome the ten canoes when they arrived at Quesnel … Roy Jackson, captain of the Simon Fraser canoe and the B.C. team, said the crews were maintaining a steady 54 strokes a minute and were making 15 miles an hour downstream.

Immediately after the sprint, the canoes were taken to the park where a painter went to work painting the names of the provinces on their sides. This made it easy for onlookers to cheer for their favourite team.

From Quesnel, the canoes were hauled over 322 kilometres (200 miles) to avoid the worst rapids through the Cariboo country. Probably the most dangerous portion of the trip was the 24-kilometre (15-mile) stretch between Yale and Hope, with the worst water at American Rock, 8 kilometres (5 miles) north of Hope. The Manitoba team set a record during this portion of the trip with a rate of 64 strokes per minute. This was a stroke rate that was difficult for the paddlers to maintain.

The going got rough when the paddlers made the jaunt across Georgia Strait to Capilano Island, where the Quebec team took a dunking in the choppy waves. They got going again and the Manitoba captain, Norm Crerar of Flin Flon, kept their spirits up by announcing that his team was getting stronger every day. He remarked, "You can bet we are looking hard at the $1,000 first prize."

According to Bill Blackburn, because of bad weather the canoes had to be pulled from the water on the last leg to Victoria.

The *Prince George Citizen* noted:

Manitoba Wins It All

A team of husky young paddlers from Manitoba won the Canadian Centennial Canoe Race from Fort St. James to Victoria. Salt-caked and bronzed after ten days of voyageuring, they led the pack into Victoria's inner harbour on the evening of August 15 by 25 minutes. B.C. finished

The BC team 1966 — Back row, left to right: Dick Hart, Harry Schwartz, Bill Blackburn, Dave Hentges and captain Roy Jackson. Front row: Herbe Brade, Costo Bush, Herb Sievers and Harvey Fraser Photo Courtesy Bill Blackburn.

Voyageurs sprinting at Yale, BC. Photo Bill Blackburn.

in second place with the others following in this order: Alberta, Quebec, Saskatchewan, Ontario, Nova Scotia, The Yukon, New Brunswick and Northwest Territories.

Immediately after the race, three members of the Northwest Territories team asked for leave to return home. Team captain Jack Adderly stated that he had obtained access to one of the men's diaries and found a repeated statement day after day, "Lonely as hell! Lonely as hell! Lonely as hell!" Adderly said all team members were trappers from north of the Arctic Circle, some of them making their first trip south. "They are all married and they just wanted to go home. They were happiest in their canoes; let loose at night in those big hotels, they were lost. They did not like the city life." The three men returned home and left their team mates to go on to Montreal for further canoe races.

Hot on the heels of the 950-kilometre (600-mile) Victoria race, the 90 paddlers and their canoes were sent to Montreal where they embarked on a seven-day canoe race to New York City. These races were a lead-up to the 100-day centennial race from Rocky Mountain House to Montreal the following year.

The winning Manitoba team. Photo Bill Blackburn.

On August 22, 1966, the ten teams of Voyageurs left Montreal on their 692-kilometre (430-mile) race to New York. BC took the first heat, but then Manitoba came through for the lead. With sprints every day along the way, they arrived in New York a week later and Manitoba took first prize. The canoeists took full advantage of their time in New York, where they had their pictures taken with the Statue of Liberty as well as alongside a huge warship. The countless memories these men amassed would stay with them throughout their lives.

THE BIG RACE — ROCKY MOUNTAIN HOUSE TO MONTREAL FOR EXPO '67

On Wednesday May 24, 1967, ten canoes loaded with Voyageurs left Rocky Mountain House, Alberta, and headed along the watery track of the old fur traders. Their destination was Montreal, 5,282 kilometres (3,283 miles) distant, with 104 days allotted for the trip.

On the previous run in 1966 the Manitoba team had advantages, such as staying in motels or hotels at night. This was not to be allowed for the '67 run, which gave it a semblance of fair play. Each team had nine paddlers with six in the canoe at all times. The other three rested and were responsible for hauling all the equipment to the camping spots, setting up and preparing meals. For this trip the BC crew was joined by Adolf Teufele and Dick Hart. Bill Blackburn came along as commodore.

Bill's job was to provide a direct line of communication with Chief Voyageur Bill Mathews, who was in charge of the race. As well, he discussed each day of travel with the BC captain, Roy "Baldy" Jackson, and the other captains, so that all were aware of what to expect during each day of travel. He also kept them abreast of danger areas and, along with the three spares, met them at camping spots with all their gear and set up camps for them. Bill was my main source of information and I put his lengthy scrapbook to good and frequent use.

The prize money was worth striving for: the total for the winning team, including sprint prizes, was estimated at $22,500. The second-place team got about $18,000, and third place, $13,500. Other teams completing the journey earned about $9,000.

The 168-kilogram (370-pound) canoes were off in a blaze of energy. Once again Manitoba set the pace but BC remained only one canoe-length behind all the way down the stretch to the water. By the time they reached the first set of rapids BC had dropped back 9 metres (30 feet), 160 metres (175 yards) ahead of Quebec. Looking at it from the bright side, one writer noted that they only had to make another four million paddle strokes and they would be at Expo. Ahead of the paddlers were another 90 stops where all manner of welcomes awaited them.

Voyageurs in New York Harbor with warship. Photo Bill Blackburn.

MAY 24 — Rocky Mountain House to Alder Flats. In the first leg of the race BC was leading Manitoba by 4.5 seconds, but no sprint was planned. Despite heavy rainfall and vehicles sliding into ditches, 3,000 people attended the fair. When everybody is at home, there are 180 people in town, but as the Voyageurs churned into sight along the North Saskatchewan River—their muscles aching from the first 77 kilometres (48 miles) and their clothing wet—more than 450 people cheered them from the shore. They stood there, dripping in the rain, the more dapper spectators with their rubber boot tops turned down, watching as the BC entry finished the first leg with a lead of four seconds. Commodore Bill Blackburn was elated at their lead over Manitoba, which most canoeists considered the team to beat.

MAY 25 — To Drayton Valley, 61 kilometres (38 miles). Sprint won by Alberta, with Manitoba second.

MAY 26 — To Devon, 137 kilometres (85 miles). Four thousand people lined the riverbank. Sprint won by Manitoba, with Saskatchewan second. A steak barbecue was enjoyed by all the paddlers, just one of countless magnificent meals that they were met with in their stops along the way.

MAY 27 — To Edmonton. Received a royal greeting from her Royal Highness Princess Alexandra, cousin to the Queen, and her husband Angus Ogilvy. He started the sprint with a gunshot, and after many errors and much confusion, Manitoba placed first, Alberta second, and BC third.

Voyageurs with the Statue of Liberty. Photo courtesy Bill Blackburn.

BC's team commodore Bill Blackburn. Photo courtesy Bill Blackburn.

Princess Alexandra appeared to enjoy every minute of attention lavished on her by the burly woodsmen. She expressed her desire to ride in one of the canoes, but wiser minds prevailed when they considered the nightmare scenario that would ensue if the canoe flipped in the North Saskatchewan River. The princess eagerly mixed with the Voyageurs, spending five minutes talking to Thomas Ross of Aklavik, a member of the Northwest Territories team. She appeared shocked when he told her that he had eleven children. Day after day, all along the rivers, the colour was spectacular as people dressed in Klondike Days' gear greeted the canoeists.

MAY 28 — To Fort Saskatchewan. A spectacular parade was staged in their honour with medallions presented by the Sherritt Gordon Refinery. The competition was controlled and canoes kept together along the route by means of timed races between given points. The team with the best total elapsed time was the winner. BC held on to second place with Manitoba holding the lead, and they won the sprint of the day.

MAY 29 — Smoky Lake. The accumulated canoe standings:

Manitoba	28:49:10
British Columbia	28:51:04
Alberta	29:34:08
Saskatchewan	29:22:03
New Brunswick	29:31:27
Ontario	29:35:07
Quebec	29:38:26
Yukon	28:47:04
NWT	30:19:25
Nova Scotia	30:33:13

The race start at Rocky Mountain House, Alberta. Photo courtesy Bill Blackburn.

If ever these men were to use foul language, it would have been along the North Saskatchewan River. Time and again they found their canoes hung up on sandbars that were difficult to spot in the murky water. By the time they realized they were on a bar, it was too late to avoid and so they had to get out and wade again and again. By the time they reached the three-quarter mark of the day's race, Alberta was leading until they misread the water and got into shallows. Once again it was BC in first with Manitoba second. This left Manitoba with a scant three-minute lead overall.

That evening several communities got together and put on a splendid show, capped with a Ukrainian supper supplied to over 1,500 people. Dancing in the streets as well as in the halls put an end to a memorable visit.

MAY 30 — To Two Hills. What had been anticipated as an easy jaunt of 50 kilometres (30 miles) turned into a hell of a test for the crews. Having the current in their favour was lost when they ran into powerful headwinds with waves up to 1 metre (3 feet) high. The worst was yet to come, as they learned when a black cloud dropped a mountain of dust on the entire area. It took about nine hours of hard work to reach their objective, where they found 8,000 dust-covered people awaiting them. In spite of the dust, a sprint was held and won by BC. Alberta was second, followed by Manitoba. Former Canadian prime minister John Diefenbaker was the guest speaker to a crowd estimated as high as 25,000 people. Among the

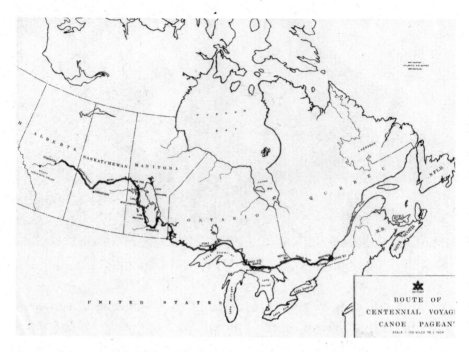

A map of the route the Centennial Voyageurs paddled and portaged to Expo '67. Courtesy Bill Blackburn.

many forms of entertainment staged for the paddlers was a special fight between members of the Cree and Blackfoot tribes. CF-104 jets from Cold Lake staged a flyby to get things underway. Performances by bands, pow-wows and smoke signals were just part of a great and memorable day. As the teams arrived at the Alberta/Saskatchewan border Manitoba was still in the lead. BC took top money in the sprint, once again showing that they were a team to be reckoned with. One canoeist expressed his gratitude by stating that he had enough memories to last many lifetimes. The music and added colour was breathtaking.

As the race moved along, it became apparent that Nova Scotia was moving out of contention. Then it became known that the Halifax Board of Trade had sponsored them but had put up no money. Consequently the team was always scrounging for supplies. Team captain John Rothwell made it plain that they were having a ball and felt no pressure whatsoever. He said that they were the only team that started out without foam or air mattresses. He added that there were always dinners for them in all the towns they stopped at and expressed his gratitude.

MAY 31 — To Elk Point. Many photographs taken along the rivers made one thing apparent—the muscles in the arms of the paddlers appeared to have increased considerably from when they started training. In fact, their physical conditioning left nothing to be desired, and they readily showed their stuff at Elk Point when a 23-year-old member of the New Brunswick team, John Murray, won a strength contest by lifting and carrying 272 kilograms (600 pounds) of salt.

The sprint was won by BC with Alberta coming in second. Manitoba placed third. Once again the Voyageurs were treated like royalty with a parade of 40 floats, costumes galore and three dances in the evening.

JUNE 1 — To Lloydminster where the Alberta–Saskatchewan border runs right through town. A pleasant surprise was the donation of a pair of jeans and jackets from GWG to each paddler. The jeans were desperately needed because the paddlers were wearing them out at a rapid rate. Every 30 strokes they slid across the canoe and changed sides. This played hell with their jeans as well as the seat covers in the canoes. A member of the sprint-winning Manitoban team received a pair of mukluks from the local newspaper editor.

JUNE 2 — To Pine Island. Manitoba won the sprint again.

JUNE 3 — To North Battleford, so named because of the memorable First Nations' battle between the Cree and Blackfoot. Again and again the paddlers learned new swear words as they fought the windswept river

Onlookers along the rivers watch the team from the Northwest Territories. Photo courtesy Bill Blackburn.

water that hid the sandbars until they were stuck on them. Manitoba came first in the sprint with Alberta and BC right behind them. Travel time indicated that the canoes were averaging 10.4 kilometres (6.5 miles) per hour on flat water; this meant they were moving at least 16 kilometres (10 miles) per hour going downstream. A necessary rest of ten minutes each hour gave the crews a chance to recuperate and be ready to ply the paddles again.

JUNE 4 — To Saskatoon. Manitoba won the sprint, beating BC again. There was now no doubt that they were the favoured team. All told, they had the most top-notch canoe men. Something that stood out time and again was just how much the Voyageurs were overwhelmed by the lavish receptions that greeted them. "Words failed them" was a common theme used by the accompanying reporters. Often the paddlers arrived wet, sore and tired, yet they were usually the first on the dance floor, ready to show their stuff.

The cycle was endless; as one newspaper noted, "Parades and dancing, singing and dining, pancakes and pow-wows, and, always, the racing."

JUNE 5 — Finally a day off to rest and repair canoes, gather up supplies and catch up on world affairs. At this point, Nova Scotia was last, 4 hours and 39 minutes behind Manitoba, whose total running time was 71 hours, 1 minute and 32 seconds since race start. BC won the sprint.

JUNE 6 — To Fort Carlton. Manitoba played tag with BC all along the river where both took turns getting stuck on sandbars.

JUNE 7 — To Prince Albert. Canoes repeatedly stuck on sandbars. Crews got out and ran, pulling the canoes as fast as possible. Manitoba won the sprint.

JUNE 8 — Day off.

JUNE 9 — To Gronlid Ferry. Manitoba appeared to be getting stronger, as they came in over ten minutes ahead of Ontario and BC.

JUNE 10 — To Nipawin, where they had to portage around the dam. They were treated to a steak supper in the middle of nowhere.

JUNE 11 — To Squaw Rapids Dam and Lake Tobin. Only a short portage around the dam.

JUNE 12 — To Cumberland House. Groups of Natives from around the Cumberland House area met the Voyageurs and treated them to an original-style meal consisting of moose meat, sturgeon, chili con carne, salads and pies.

JUNE 13 — To The Pas, Manitoba. Perhaps it was the green moose meat eaten the day before, but the day had been spent in agony for many of the paddlers. The canoes were repeatedly hauled up the bank so the men could relieve themselves. The Yukon team claimed they held the record for toilet paper consumption. One official noted that unlike traditional meals, this one did not stick to the ribs.

JUNE 15 AND 16 — The Pas to Mossy Portage. Had trouble with high winds in Cedar Lake and had to lay up for hours. When the crews were ordered to line up for a race they refused, and the officials finally gave up the idea. Finally got through the 7-kilometre (4.5–mile) portage to Lake Winnipegosis.

JUNE 17 — To Duck Bay. Paddlers had a terrible time with wind and waves. It took almost 12 hours to cross to Duck Bay where they stayed over and rested up. Nova Scotia was dead last, and then their man Rothwell came up with a splendid idea. He got a 6V battery and pump, hooked it up in their canoe and it worked like a charm. Soon they were pulling away from the others who were constantly bailing to keep their canoes from swamping. In no time at all the other canoes were sporting

BC and Manitoba finishing a sprint. Photo courtesy Steve Schwartz.

the same device. Surprisingly, the New Brunswick team won the sprint and the $100 that went with it.

JUNE 19 — From Lake Winnipegosis 24 kilometres (15 miles) through to Meadow Portage. Because Manitoba was always in the lead, the other teams followed them. On this occasion it was to their sorrow, as they went the wrong way. Someone put the marker flag in the wrong place and only BC found the proper course and went directly to Meadow Portage. This gave them a 45-minute lead on Manitoba.

The newspapers noted, "The early lead gained by Manitoba in the first days of the epic cross-country canoe race to Expo 67 was wiped out by BC by Tuesday afternoon, with 36 seconds of paddling time separating the two teams. BC took the lead in the 15-mile trip from Winnipegosis to the settlement of Meadow Portage at the northern end of Lake Winnipegosis."

According to eyewitnesses, BC paddlers were on shore just killing themselves with laughter when the other teams finally arrived.

Commodore Bill Blackburn told me, "It really inspired us to beat the great Manitoba team in their backyard." The canoes were brigaded

Steve Schwartz leads BC team across a portage. Photo courtesy Bill Blackburn.

across a 3-kilometre (2-mile) portage from Lake Winnipegosis to Lake Manitoba and then paddled on to Crane River on June 20. Worth mentioning is that the idea to copy the fur-trader canoes proved to be a good one when they faced and bettered waves up to 3.6 metres (12 feet) on Lake Winnipegosis. A launch followed the canoes in case of an accident, but the stable, durable crafts made it through without any assistance.

The Manitoba team, in their canoe named *Radisson*, did great until they made that grave error. The wrong turn lost them their 41-minute lead, and BC, formerly in second place, ended up with a 36-second lead. Was there any hanky-panky involved? There was even an official timer at the wrong spot to greet Manitoba. They protested but to no avail. Not quitters, the 'Tobans, as they were referred to, were back with a 23-minute lead within two days because of another strange development.

JUNE 21 — Crane River to Lake Manitoba Narrows. Manitoba appeared to be in a class by themselves on the big lakes. Hence on the 88-kilometre (55-mile) run, they ended up back in first place again having beaten BC by over 22 minutes.

JUNE 22 — To Bruce Beach. Manitoba set the pace again.

JUNE 23 — To Dauphin. Just a short run and then some time off, which was always welcomed by the whole gang.

JUNE 24 — To Rainbow Beach. The 'Tobans won the sprint with Alberta second and BC third.

JUNE 25 — To Delta. The teams reached Delta and then for some strange reason all the canoes took a wrong turn except the 'Tobans. Since it was their province, one cannot help but wonder if a little revenge came down the pipe, because the 'Tobans ended up with an hour and a half lead.

It didn't take long to smell a rat, because Manitoba, the team always in the lead, was lagging behind that day. That was the reason they were not followed by the other teams. With that 90-minute lead, trying to catch a powerful team like Manitoba was probably considered mission impossible. Surely it must have taken the steam out of the other teams.

Describing the incident, Commodore Bill Blackburn noted, "The canoes were three miles offshore, heading along the same course when Manitoba turned toward a tower on shore. The rest of the pageant kept going straight on. Later, the Manitoba team indicated they had known the tower was near the finishing point, a fact the other teams hadn't been told."

On June 26, the Voyageurs reached Portage la Prairie, a tough 30-kilometre (19-mile) jaunt through the woods. Teams were allowed to use any method of transport that was available 100 years earlier. Some used horses and carts, but New Brunswick went a step further and hired six local First Nations women to carry their canoe. Alberta and Quebec showed what they were made of by carrying their canoes the entire distance.

JUNE 27 – One of the highlights of the trip awaited them at Winnipeg, where they took a couple of days off. They stayed over for a sumptuous feast on July 1. Almost one ton of lobsters had been flown in from the Maritimes. A monster cake was the capper and then an estimated 30,000 people watched as BC won the sprint of the day. As was the rule, prizes of $30 to about $400 were given to the winning team of each sprint; this helped enormously with expenses, and the sprints added a lot of colour and excitement to the festivities at each community.

JULY 1 — At Winnipeg. Among the show-and-tell was a strength demonstration by king trapper Roger Carrière of the Manitoban team. He impressed onlookers by carrying 330 kilograms (725 pounds) of salt.

JULY 2 — To Fort Gary. The 'Tobans won the sprint over BC by two seconds; how close can you get?

JULY 3 — To Winnipeg Beach. Out of the Red River and into Lake Winnipeg where winds were a problem. BC won the sprint.

JULY 4 — To Pine Falls where the lake run brought out some different sprint winners. Manitoba was first, winning $500. Ontario was second, and then Alberta and BC.

JULY 5 — To Lac du Bonnet. Voyageurs faced five portages and then were in for a history lesson. The name Lac du Bonnet got its origin back in 1731 when the voyageur de la Vérendrye arrived. One story says that he tossed his hat into the air and it landed in a tree. Then he was greeted by an Indian princess, Minnewawa, whom he kissed, so he named the lake Lac du Bonnet because he had lost his hat to a tree. The teams learned another thing about this little town. They found the town had a mascot called the Mugwump. This encouraged a wise guy to quip, "The Mugwump is a mighty strange mother; its mug is found on one end and its wump is on the other."

This 48-kilometre (30-mile) trip on the Winnipeg River was no piece of cake. With its five portages, fighting the·current and a strong headwind, it made for a tough day.

JULY 6 — To Pinawa. Another portage and the 'Tobans won the sprint and $100. Strange to say, New Brunswick was second.

JULY 7 — To Point du Bois. Another two portages. BC won the sprint. After fighting strong winds and high waves, the paddlers were beat and in need of a rest.

JULY 8 — To Boundary Island. Another portage but canoeists finally entered Ontario.

JULY 9 — To Minaki. Manitoba holding a 1 hour and 40 minute lead over BC with Alberta third.

JULY 10 — To Kenora by way of yet another portage. Manitoba won the sprint with BC in second and Yukon third.

Teams had to portage around Norman Dam. Kenora was the end of the 10-day trip up the Winnipeg River. Canadian Secretary of State Judy LaMarsh greeted and acknowledged the importance of the teams' efforts.

JULY 11 — To Sand Point Reserve. Teams faced huge waves on the 72-kilometre (45-mile) lap to the Indian reserve. Manitoba had a 36-hour lead over last-place Nova Scotia at this point. When queried as to how they went to the bathroom out on the big lakes, one paddler said, "Number one was easy, we just used a bucket; number two was tricky but we just hung out over the side of the canoe and mooned the fleet."

JULY 12 — To Rainy River. Voyageurs faced 3.5-metre (12-foot) waves on Lake of the Woods and made some time by staying in the shelter of many small islands. Eventually they were forced to take shelter for five hours on Bigsby Island. According to the canoeists, the waves were still as much as 2.5 metres (8 feet) high when they resumed their race. Then they moved on to Rainy River and crossed to the settlement of Beadette, Minnesota, where they were cordially greeted by William O'Brien representing Governor Harold LeVander. Possibly the highlight of the trip was the warm reception afforded them in Minnesota. The governor even went so far as to name an island in Saganaga Lake after them. Named Norwester Island, it was a tribute to the many that followed in the footsteps of the pioneers.

JULY 13 — To Emo and Fort Frances. The Rainy River weaves back and forth along the border between Ontario and Minnesota. From there they moved up the river through two sets of the dangerous Manitou Rapids. Some teams were forced to track their canoes through the rapids, using a line from shore. The next stop was Emo, Ontario. On July 13 they made the 48 kilometres (30 miles) to Fort Frances and totalled about one mile of portaging.

JULY 14 — To Fort Frances, where the crews took the Voyageurs' oath that they would never kiss another Voyageur's wife without her permission. They were duly initiated as Norwesters and granted licence to the red cap and black plume. This was followed by a stiff drink of Caribou, which was a potent mix of wine, brandy and grain alcohol. At this point the crews were getting ready to enter the Quetico Park system, home of the famous Native pictographs. This area has often been described as "supernatural" by its visitors. During their three days of isolation in Quetico Park the paddlers had to carry their own bedrolls and supplies.

JULY 15— Fort Frances to Crane Lake through three tough portages. Tiny creeks between small lakes made for rough going.

BE IT KNOWN BY THESE PRESENTS THAT

BILL BLACKBURN

IS PROCLAIMED

VoyAGEUR

IN THE

INTERNATIONAL ORDER OF CANOE COUNTRY TRAVELLERS

QUETICO-SUPERIOR CANOE AREA

HON. RENE BRUNELLE
Minister, Ontario Department
of Lands and Forests, Canada

ORVILLE L. FREEMAN
Secretary of Agriculture
United States of America

Bill Blackburn's Quetico/Superior Park membership. Courtesy Bill Blackburn.

JULY 16 — To Lac la Croix. Paddlers thoroughly enjoyed the trip through the park. All were carrying their campout gear, which made it tough with the extra weight. The campouts were a chance to get to know the others much better. This was meant to test the mettle of the crews as they faced over three miles of portaging. A special event took place when a plane flew in food for an evening meal. Talk about roughing it!

They surely did rough it in some respects. Apparently the mosquitoes were unbearable. One paddler described how he had to tie the bottom of his pant legs to stop the 'skitters from crawling up his legs. The effort failed because while he would tie off one leg, the mosquitoes would untie the other.

JULY 17 — To Table Rock. Teams held a sprint from Atikokan, Ontario, to Ely, Minnesota. All teams seemed to enjoy the park, with one exception—the crews were solidly against including the portages in the race time. Perhaps as a way of showing their resentment, they rigged a race. This led to a rather strange report coming out of Ely. A 48-kilometre (30-mile) sprint across a waterway appropriately known as Crooked Lake came to a shocking conclusion. The last two canoes almost tied for first place and the top four canoes tied for last place. This defied logic and it appeared obvious that a bit of good sportsmanship had taken place, or it was a sign of rebellion. One mystified official noted, "How can four canoes tie? It is impossible; there would be at least a fraction of a second difference in their times."

When the teams were camped near Ely, one of the Voyageurs allowed that it seemed like they had been paddling forever; this led an official to make his day by notifying them that they had just reached the halfway point in the race.

JULY 18 — All Voyageurs stopped and studied the world-famous Native rock paintings and then slogged their way through a couple of portages. Since their canoes were loaded with all their campout gear, this brought the weight of their burden to over 230 kilograms (500 pounds).

To Baylay Bay. Again, until it got tiring, the 'Tobans beat BC in the sprint. No doubt about it, Manitoba was always the team to beat. But from their point of view, it was always BC that was the team to beat.

JULY 19 — To Norwester Island, the renamed island in Saganaga Lake on the Minnesota side of the river. Terribly tough day for the paddlers with six portages through an endless series of lakes. This area was once described to me by a forest ranger: "It has to be seen to be believed; stunning panoramas of mountains, lakes, rivers and portages." It is one of the premier canoeing spots with thousands of visitors each summer.

JULY 20 — To Gunflint Lake. Eight more tough portages. 'Tobans beat BC again in the sprint.

JULY 21 — To Mountain Lake through seven portages, where all Voyageurs participated in the "Height of Land Ceremony." They again took a stiff drink of Caribou, giving them the necessary courage to take the Oath of the Voyageurs.

This was a rough day with one portage after another. BC and the 'Tobans assisted each other in portaging their canoes; this helped enormously.

JULY 22 — To Partridge Falls. The crews finally got into the Partridge River and had to deal with low water, rapids and rocks on the way to the falls. Another workout day with seven portages.

JULY 23 — The mighty Grand Portage — 15 kilometres (9.5 miles) of back-breaking labour in the portages. Made it to Grand Portage on Lake Superior. Of obvious concern was that these men were using 8-metre (26-foot) canoes, while the original voyageurs used 11-metre (36-foot)

Stockade at Grand Portage. Photo courtesy Bill Blackburn.

vessels on the big water (Superior). Grand Portage, Minnesota, is home to a stockade with a great hall and gatehouse, which was reconstructed on the site of the old North West Company depot.

JULY 24 — To Thunder Bay. About 2,500 people gathered to watch the ten canoes glide out of the mist and head across the dreaded Lake Superior. Escorted by two ships and a Coast Guard cutter, they found the lake surprisingly calm. Several extra days were allotted for dealing with heavy seas on Superior, but day after day the Voyageurs were greatly surprised to find calm water. Because of this, several planned stops were cancelled and they arrived in Black Wharf 24 hours ahead of time. Many times the compasses acted up, probably because of the abundance of iron ore in the area.

JULY 25 — A blessed day off for all. Often these spare moments were used to catch up on laundry and things of that nature.

JULY 26 — Stayed over in Thunder Bay. BC beat the 'Tobans in the sprint.

JULY 27 — The canoes were out on the water two hours before day-light; their intent was to avoid the heavy winds that came up later in the day. All the men had to follow was a glow on the horizon. Once again the mighty Superior was surprisingly calm. In 14 hours of paddling the men covered almost 160 kilometres (100 miles) and made it to Red Rock 24 hours ahead of time.

JULY 28 AND 29 — The crews holed up at Red Rock and played games, relaxed, danced and dined. BC won the sprint with the 'Tobans coming in second.

JULY 30 — 72 kilometres (45 miles) to Terrace Bay. Another beauti-ful day with the mighty Superior peacefully at rest.

JULY 31 — Another day off to play games and rest up.

AUGUST 1 — In Terrace Bay with another day off.

AUGUST 2 — To Marathon. Met two safety ships out in the fog; five canoes followed behind each ship. The foghorns were blasting to the point that it became annoying. Large waves made it interesting and, according to BC commodore Bill Blackburn, the fog was so misleading that they got turned around and had a time finding the other canoes. The safety ships were bobbing up and down as well as the canoes so this resulted in a group of seasick paddlers. And the eternal fog that seemed to hide everything from view hid the horizon and gave them no sense of positional awareness.

AUGUST 3 — Day off.

AUGUST 4 — To a secluded beach along Lake Superior.

AUGUST 5 — To Michipikoten.

AUGUST 6 — To Wawa. A day off in what the Voyageurs described as the spot where, "if someone wanted to give the world an enema, that is where they would insert the tube." The centennial banquet was arranged so that the Voyageurs would pay for the food. One of the diners suspected that the moose meat they ate was roadkill.

AUGUST 8 — To Agawa Bay. Another eight hours of paddling behind the ships.

AUGUST 9 — To Pancake Bay. More fog out on the lake. Fortunately the ships had radar, which picked up the aluminum paddles the canoeists were using. Manitoba was ahead two hours overall.

AUGUST 10 — To Sault Ste. Marie. Faced with large waves but made the 72-kilometre (45-mile) trip with only minor problems.

AUGUST 11 — Day off.

AUGUST 12 — Went through the locks and had a sprint. The 'Tobans beat BC again.

AUGUST 13 — To Thessalon. More of the same. 'Tobans won the sprint.

AUGUST 14 — To Blind River. Crews really pigged out and then danced with what little energy was left. Sprint won by 'Tobans with BC a close second.

AUGUST 15 — To Little Current on Manitoulin Island. An 88-kilometre (55-mile) jaunt across the top of Georgian Bay. Manitoba came first in the sprint, with Alberta second and BC third.

AUGUST 16 — Day off. Sprint had the same ending.

AUGUST 17 — To French River. All across the tip of Georgian Bay the Voyageurs faced what their original namesakes had dealt with; waves 4 to 5 metres (15 to 18 feet) high continually breaking all around them and making the noise of a freight train. To the joy of all involved, the huge waves of 320-kilometre-long (200-mile) Lake Huron were finally behind them. The naval escort fired flares and displayed a farewell sign as the canoes headed up the French River. After all the time the canoe and naval men had spent together, it must have been an emotional parting. Alberta had decided to follow the shoreline in the lee of islands. Even there they ran into waves 2.5 metres (8 feet) high and were an extra couple of hours arriving in camp.

In some places the teams fought huge waves. Photo courtesy Bill Blackburn.

For those Voyageurs who had never been on huge lakes before this trip, a new experience was in store for them—paddling against a strong side wind. This was demanding of the men in the bow and stern. The canoes continually wanted to wind-cock and thus had to be fought to keep on track. As I have spent a lot of time canoeing and learned to love it, I also remember being dog-tired after fighting a side wind for hours on end. When paddling alone against a side wind, I found it impossible to prevent wind-cocking unless I put a weight in the front of the canoe to prevent it from turning.

AUGUST 18 — On the French River. There was one portage around a 12-metre (40-foot) waterfall; other than that the crews enjoyed the scenic route along the river. The downside of this trip was the narrow defile between the rock cliffs on both sides of the river. At times there was barely enough room to paddle without hitting the banks with their paddles. They spent the night at Schell's Camp near Sudbury, and the 'Tobans won the sprint over BC.

AUGUST 19 — At Schell's Camp with a day off. Sprint won by 'Tobans with Quebec second and BC third.

AUGUST 20 — To Dokis on Lake Nipissing. Voyageurs spent the day fighting six sets of rapids with some portages. Three crews managed to fight their way up the rapids but the others gave up and had to portage.

AUGUST 21 — To North Bay. When the teams approached the finish line, it was hidden behind a little island. As luck would have it, Saskatchewan was in a race with Nova Scotia and decided to take a shortcut on the inside passage of an island. It turned out to be the wrong way and the prairie boys found themselves grounded on a sandbar. They picked up the canoe and ran with it to the finish line, only to find that they had left a member of their crew out on the bar. They beat the Scotians to the finish line but then had to stop rejoicing and go back to the bar to retrieve their mate. Then the canoes were moved to nearby Trout Lake where a sprint was quickly organized. Same two winners, but it ended in a photo finish for Manitoba and British Columbia, consistently the two top racers in the pageant.

AUGUST 22 — Day off.

AUGUST 23 — To Mattawa. Because of the low water levels the paddlers were faced with a dozen portages. BC won the sprint. The undersides of the canoes took a beating from scraping the rock in the river bottom. They needed a lot of attention, such as waxing.

AUGUST 24 — To Stonecliffe Park on the Ottawa River. Not a fun day by any standards as the crews faced a dozen portages. The men were treated to a fine meal. 'Tobans won the sprint.

AUGUST 25 — To Deep River. 'Tobans won again.

AUGUST 26 — To Pembroke. Paddlers learned what the original voyageurs had to face when they fought their way through thick fog. 'Tobans again won the sprint.

Quesnel's *Cariboo Observer* noted on August 26:

> Most of the tough ones are behind them now as the Centennial voyageurs head onto the home stretch. The flotilla of ten crews was due at Riverside Park in Pembroke at 3:30 p.m. today ... only eight more days to go and their epic 3,283-mile journey which started last May 24 from Rocky Mountain House in Alberta, will be over when they swoop triumphantly into the marina at Expo September 4.
>
> It's been a long time and a long haul away from families for some of them, but the Voyageurs appear as enthusiastic and as pleased with their roles as they were

when I first had the opportunity to talk with them just a year ago in New York City.

The Voyageurs still talk about the reception there. Vic Chapman, project officer with the teams, says the reception in New York, where they staged their eastern trial run from Expo to New York Harbour, was second to none, despite the spectacular attention they have been getting at nearly every stop along the way this year. Three Canadian destroyers formed part of the escort that day up the Hudson River to the Statue of Liberty where the Voyageurs placed a wreath on the water, boat whistles blared and the New York fireboat saluted the Canadians with 40-foot streams of water soaring skyward in the late summer haze; an honor reserved for only a few.

AUGUST 27 — To Campbell's Bay. A few rapids were dealt with as the crews finally entered Quebec and the last stages of their epic journey. BC and Alberta won the sprint.

AUGUST 28 — To Arnprior. Crews faced heavy rain almost all day. There were a dozen portages along the Ottawa River. Everything was back to normal as 'Tobans won the sprint with Ontario and BC following.

AUGUST 29 — To Ottawa. The canoes had to be taken through a 1-kilometre portage by Chatt Falls. The next day a headline noted:

A Large Crowd of 7000 Greet Centennial Voyageurs at Ottawa

The Centennial voyageurs, brown as the beaver furs their forebears carried down the Ottawa River a century and more ago, splashed ashore at the capital Tuesday ... Today they are to be received by Governor-General Michener and later are to haul their 10 canoes on to Parliament Hill for a welcome by Prime Minister Pearson.

The prime minister told them that if all Canadians could show the kind of cooperation within Canada that the paddlers had shown during this trip "we would have no difficulties." He added that he had considered sending a cabinet canoe with the pageant down the Ottawa River to Expo: "I was going to put it in charge of Miss LaMarsh, but she couldn't find another cabinet minister in good enough shape to go with her."

AUGUST 30 — To Hull. Extremely shallow water caused some damage to the bottoms of the canoes, but with the ability of the canoeists, they were soon repaired and ready for the challenges ahead.

AUGUST 31 — To Plaisance. Only one portage to deal with, but this led to a surprising outcome in the sprint: Ontario, Quebec, BC, Manitoba and then Alberta.

SEPTEMBER 1 — To Hawksbury. BC given a penalty, which resulted in their being placed ninth in the sprint; 'Tobans came first again.

SEPTEMBER 2 — To Carillon. Hydro splurged and supplied a supper of Cornish game hen.

SEPTEMBER 3 — To Lachine. Sprint won by BC with Alberta on their tail. 'Tobans came third. Crews had a rough time with the shale-covered river bottoms. The sharp rock was a constant threat to the canoes, but the shallow water left little options for the canoeists. At last they arrived in the St. Lawrence River where they had their hands full with the treacherous Lachine Rapids. The Yukon swamped and had to be assisted by escorting boats. Another canoe took too much water and had to be towed to shore and bailed out before it could continue.

SEPTEMBER 4 — To Expo, Montreal. The final sprint was taken at the man-made Regatta Lake on the Expo site, and perhaps it was appropriate that Manitoba won. BC was second and that was no surprise either. This mirrored the trend that had developed all along the waterways of the cross-Canada race during which Manitoba had built up a lead that was impossible to overtake. Judy LaMarsh gave engraved watches to each of the winning team members.

⌣

Memories of this fantastic trip were numerous. All along the waterways the men were treated to different and exotic types of food, such as at Mattawa where a wild game cook prepared muktuk (whale blubber), beaver tail loaf and bear roast. Another feast included beaver, blood pudding, moose and Arctic char.

Each man on the winning Manitoba team got $2,500 for the 5,282-kilometre (3,283-mile) race, while those on the second-place BC team received $2,000. Third place got $1,500, and $1,000 went to each

A feast awaited the paddlers in Quebec. Photo courtesy Bill Blackburn.

person completing the race. I asked Bill Blackburn why Manitoba won the overall race and he left me with the impression that it was a combination of things. To start with, they had several professional canoeists who had won many individual races. As well, they had much in the way of experience and they practised hard.

There are many things for a canoeist to consider. One must be able to read the water. If there's a riffle in the water ahead, it could be caused by a rock or submerged log. Other important aspects of racing are smoothing off scratches on the bottoms of the canoes, which act as a drag. Some canoeists spent their spare time faithfully waxing their canoes so they would glide with less friction. One thing is certain in canoeing: as with

The final official times for the centennial cross-Canada canoe race were:

Manitoba — 531 hours 6 minutes 16 seconds
British Columbia — 532 hours 26 minutes 14 seconds
Alberta — 535 hours 19 minutes 30 seconds
Ontario — 537 hours 55 minutes 46 seconds
New Brunswick — 540 hours 12 minutes 44 seconds
Saskatchewan — 541 hours 47 minutes 41 seconds
Quebec — 544 hours 3 minutes 57 seconds
Northwest Territories — 547 hours 55 minutes 53 seconds
Yukon Territory — 558 hours 40 minutes 54 seconds
Nova Scotia — 566 hours 4 minutes 20 seconds

The time difference between first and last was 34 hours 58 minutes 4 seconds.

a chain, it is only as strong as its weakest link. It seems that Manitoba's weakest link was fairly strong. This was not the case with some of the other teams. For instance, while commenting on his team's less than satisfactory showing in the race, Gill Tinkler of the Quebec team stated, "I didn't agree with the final choice of the team. Bob Codner and Jimmy Perez were champions of kayak racing, but that doesn't necessarily mean that they are champions of the canoe. They could only do endurance competitions for a while, 15 minutes or so, but not for four or six hours. I think we came in seventh today because of this."

I was pleasantly surprised to learn that not one fatality took place during all the training and the races combined. Regrettably, Dick Hart of Prince George was drowned in the Bow River a few years later. But most surprising was that in all the thousands of miles covered, not one canoe was seriously damaged. The spare canoe that had been taken along for such an event was never used in the race. This speaks volumes about the professionalism of these men. The canoes did take a severe beating nonetheless, especially on the portages, and by the time they reached Expo some of the names on the canoes could scarcely be recognized.

When one considers the obvious hanky-panky that went on when Manitoba took the big leap forward of 1 hour and 30 minutes on June 25, the BC team members need not hang their heads. They came in 1 hour, 19 minutes and 58 seconds behind Manitoba. This is less than the 'Tobans gained on June 25. But when we consider that the 'Tobans won most of the sprints, then perhaps they deserved the title. At the same time, I think BC did us proud.

Another thing that should be mentioned is that the Manitoba team had a secret weapon. One of their paddlers, Roger Carrière, was a brute of a man; in a strength contest at Winnipeg he carried 330 kilograms (725 pounds) of salt. I wonder how many paddles he broke! Roger was no doubt part of the reason the press repeatedly used the phrase "the husky paddlers from Manitoba."

After returning to Prince George, some of the BC crew members were honoured at a social evening in the upper Mud River district. Asa Fishback, on behalf of the gathering, extended congratulations to the group on their achievement and thanked them for their efforts, which had brought honour to their community, province and country. Voyageurs present were Harry and Steve Schwartz, Costo Bush, Dave Hentges,

Herbe Brade and Bill Blackburn. These men were not only a source of pride for BC; they also accumulated an abundance of memories that would never die. I had no trouble believing Bill when he said that this trip was the most outstanding adventure of his entire life.

After the race was over, one of the Voyageurs put it quite eloquently by saying, "All I can remember of the last three months is paddling, eating, paddling, racing, dancing, paddling, eating, signing registers, paddling; it's all a big blur but mostly it's the paddling I remember."

Bill Blackburn summed it up this way: "I don't think Manitoba's team captain, Norm Crerar, would mind me quoting him, because I think he got it right when he said, 'The entire adventure began as a dream and ended as a dream.'"

6.

ODDITIES OF NATURE

Many strange events take place in nature. Some seem so utterly cruel that they appear out of what should be the natural order. For instance, animals that encounter a porcupine in the wilds may attempt to sniff it, only to wind up with a face full of quills. This can and does lead to unimaginable suffering and death by starvation. When I was just a young lad many people used to say that porcupines could throw their quills. I don't know if they believed it or not; perhaps they told us such a story to make us stay clear of them.

Grizzly with porcupine quills. Photo Roger Scott.

During September 2009 a young grizzly was found in a disabled state near the Kemess Mine area of BC. The poor creature's curiosity must have got the better of it and it attempted to check out a porcupine. In return it ended up with a mouthful of quills. The last I heard, it had come to an inglorious end. Some animals can cope rather well with quills inside their bodies. Fishers, for example, have been found with quills in their livers, still in apparent good health. Also, it is rather common for trappers to find wolverines with quills protruding from body parts. Trapper Arna Jenson once caught a wolverine with quills protruding from one of its eyes. Although it was blind in that eye, it was still business as usual.

Buddy with porcupine quills. Photo Annie Dingwall.

A perfect example of animals not learning after being clobbered by porcupines was just given to me by Earl and Annie Dingwall of Prince George. Their dog, a friendly critter named Buddy, was cavorting with two other dogs when they met a porky and the fight was on. When the smoke cleared it was plain to see that the dogs were the decided losers. A trip to the vet was necessary to restore them to near normal, and one would assume that was the last of it, but not so. Two weeks later the same three dogs went travelling again and met another, or perhaps the same, porcupine. The end result was another trip to the vet for all three dogs. The total price for the vet was $600. And don't bet any money that it is over. I know a man whose dog was attacked four times, and the last attack was so bad, with quills in both eyes, that he had to put it down.

On December 4, 1922, Frank Pierreway of Prince George passed away in the Quesnel Hospital after an eight-day illness. An autopsy determined that death was due to peritonitis caused by a porcupine quill having punctured his intestines in several places. It is hard to imagine how this could have happened. Perhaps the man was alone at the time and the spot where the quill entered his body was out of his line of vision.

There are numerous reports of porcupine attacks on domestic animals. Pack train operator Stan Hale told me that he had to remove them from his horses every year. One mare in particular wanted to check out every porcupine it met on its travels. Invariably it would receive a snoutful of quills and Stan would have a few hours' work removing them.

⌣

My nephew David Humphreys was walking along a trail near Prince George when he had a rather strange experience with a cow moose. It started following him and since it showed no sign of anger, such as flattened ears or raised hair, he waited for it. It walked right up to him and sniffed his camera while he took a picture. Then, just as unconcerned, it walked away into the surrounding woods.

Animals can be curious to a fault, and this often gets them into trouble. My friend Eric Klaubauf had a similar visitation from a moose when he was falling timber at Driscoll Creek. Eric had stopped working to eat his lunch, and as it was a nice, sunny day, he leaned back beside a large log and was soon fast asleep. Sometime later he awoke to find a cow moose's nose about a hand width away from his own nose, perhaps trying to find out why he was remaining stationary for so long. Instantly Eric shouted and threw himself to one side. The moose did likewise and then went tearing away into the thickets. It was every bit as frightened as Eric, or perhaps even more so. Moose, deer and caribou are inquisitive to the point of being ridiculous. Case in point: One October day back in the 1950s I was hunting along a mountain ridge when I came upon a caribou pawing up moss and lichens. I was walking through a stand of large cedar trees at the time and I came within 10 metres (33 feet) of it before we spotted each other. It made a leap into the air and then stared at me with its eyes bugging out. I stood stationary and about a minute later it went back to pawing again and paid me no attention whatsoever. Imagine what chance this animal would have against a wolf pack.

I believe the main reason for the demise of the caribou populations in central BC was the arrival of wolves, which increased with the buildup of the moose populations in the 1920s and '30s. The caribou had little to no experience with wolf packs and were sitting ducks, so to speak. Perhaps I am being unkind when I suggest that caribou rank right up there with lynx as the dumbest animals in the woods.

Another time I ran into a herd of about 20 caribou on a ridge about 800 metres (2,650 feet) above the main valley. I shot one bull and the

Moose sniffing David's camera. Photo David Humphreys.

Two lynx. Photo Elmer Micks.

others left at tremendous speed. About 10 minutes later they returned at high speed and surrounded me, all of them staring as I butchered the bull. Within half a minute they tore away again at high speed and disappeared. Go figure these strange, inquisitive animals.

Paul Paulson of Prince George has a great deal of video of a cow moose that used to hang around his hunting camp at Kluachesi Lake in northern BC. Possibly driven to the camp by wolves, this creature sometimes stuck its head right inside the tent and showed no fear whatsoever. One year it brought its calf along and it too was unafraid. But the best was yet to come when rutting season started, because a bull moose appeared near the camp. For a couple of days it wandered around within 10 metres (33 feet) of the hunters. If this shows us anything, it is just how quickly wildlife can adapt to new situations.

Paul recalls the day he and his son Grant were crossing the lake in their boat when they spotted a cow moose swimming toward them. Then Grant pointed to the lakeshore where a grizzly bear was standing. Suddenly it became obvious to the men that the moose was using them for protection. It followed them right back to their camp while the grizzly went on to new adventures.

Bernard Johnson of Houston, BC, had a surprise visitor one day last summer. He was out in his yard when he spotted a young buck deer in the velvet. Bernard was just about to eat an apple when the deer walked right up to him and would have taken the apple if Bernard had not pulled it away at the last instant. Then the deer silently walked away and never returned. This raises the question, is it my imagination or are animals in general losing their fear of humans? If so, what will be the end result of this?

Bernard and a tame deer. Photo Bernard Johnson.

Clara and Hap Bowden of Quesnel, BC, who were the subjects of my book *Wilderness Dreams,* had a dog named Sparky. This dog had a running battle with a squirrel that went on for years. The squirrel would torment Sparky mercilessly until the dog would take a run at the tree the squirrel was in. Sometimes the dog would propel himself 3 or 4 metres (10 to 13 feet) up the tree before he would run out of momentum and come sliding back down again. One day the squirrel was tormenting Sparky when it lost its footing and fell from the tree. Like a flash, Sparky flew at the animal and came within inches of getting it. From that day on, Mister

Sparky climbing the tree, c. 1998. Photo Hap Bowden.

Squirrel kept a respectable distance from Sparky, and the show the Bowdens had repeatedly enjoyed came to a close.

I love watching wildlife. At times wild animals provide us with memorable performances. A friend and I were enjoying our local park when we lucked out. A tap used to water the grass was leaking and had a puddle of water around it. As we sat there, a squirrel came out of a tree and ran toward the puddle to sate its thirst. Before it got there a crow dived out of a nearby tree and chased it back to its original tree. The crow circled the tree a couple of times but had no chance of catching the fleet squirrel. At last the crow flew into a nearby tree and waited. Out came the squirrel and again the crow dived at it. We witnessed a wonderful show that went on for the better part of an hour. Several times they sat in opposing trees and cussed at each other something terrible. I believe it was all in fun, and fun it certainly was for us. By the time we moved on, the squirrel had still not managed to sate its thirst. Oh, how I longed for a camera that day!

Pilot Brian Marynovich flies a great deal and therefore gets the opportunity to take lots of pictures. One day he had an interesting time watching a squirrel that had found a can of Coca-Cola. After a great deal of effort the squirrel finally found a way to get at the pop. I had visions of the Coca-Cola company using it as an advertisement.

Animals all have weaknesses of one kind or another; some, such as mountain goats, never learned to count. I recall the time a friend and I were looking for goats along the McGregor Mountains in what I had been told was a good spot for viewing them. Sure enough, that was where we found a small herd. No sooner had I stuck my head up above the ridgetop and trained my binoculars on an adjacent ridge than, right in the centre of my field of view, a large goat appeared. Guess what it was doing? It was staring directly at me. Much the same as mountain sheep, goats are noted for having vision equal to that of a person with 7-power binoculars. I called to Eric to just keep walking at a 90 percent angle to the goat, not looking at it, and that is what we both did. When we passed through a row of timber and were out of its sight, I followed the row of trees directly toward the goat and came out a stone's throw below it. Meanwhile, Eric had kept going straight ahead and the goat was watching him with total interest, completely oblivious to my whereabouts. It seems apparent that here was one goat that never learned to count.

Because they fly so near to the ground, helicopter pilots often get close-up views of wildlife. Therefore I enjoy quizzing them about their travels and adventures. I recall a story told to me by Lee Sexsmith, who flew in the North for many years. In this case, he was flying alongside a mountain when he came upon a huge grizzly, far and away bigger than any he has seen before or since. In an effort to escape, the grizzly tore through thick alder swales at full gallop. The brush was so thick that a human could scarcely move in it and yet the grizzly galloped through it and it simply moved out of the way. Lee says it was one of the most impressive things he ever viewed.

Pilot Keith Westfall told me of a similar incident. As he was flying along in a helicopter near Tree Lake in the Northwest Territories, he came upon a herd of muskoxen. Immediately upon sighting the helicopter, they formed a circle with the young in the centre, where they were protected. But the best part was yet to come, for as Keith neared the herd a large bull left the circle and came to meet him. It had no apparent fear of this noisy creature that was posing a threat to its herd. Keith turned the helicopter away and continued with his journey, while at the same time he was decidedly impressed with the courage of that large bull.

Squirrel and Coca-Cola. Photo Brian Marynovich.

There is always an element of danger in nature. My friend Vern Goglin gave me a picture of a beaver that was killed by the tree it was falling. The events leading up to the tragedy were evident: the tree that killed the beaver got hung up in another tree, then jumped the stump and landed on top of the beaver. Possibly this is not a rare event, especially when we realize that beavers do much of their falling during the hours of darkness. Take note, also, that the beaver was not wearing a hard hat. Where is the Workers' Compensation Board when it is really needed?

Beaver killed by a tree. Photo Vern Goglin.

One of the strangest experiences of my life happened when I was on a fishing trip about 22 kilometres (14 miles) back in the mountains. Lindy Chambers and I spent three days fishing and were returning home when we encountered an exceptionally heavy rainstorm. Perhaps because we were wet and miserable, we got careless and wandered off course on a game trail. Eventually we got so turned around that we just waded through devil's club for hours. When darkness came we were forced to make camp, at which time we figured out where we had gone wrong. The next day we made our way home where I was in for a wicked surprise. When I lowered my jeans, I found I had thousands of devil's club spines in my legs, from just below my waist to the top of my hiking boots. I showed them to my father who shook his head in disbelief. For a while I was seriously worried, thinking I was certain to get an infection. What to do? I made a valiant attempt to remove them with a needle but quickly gave up because I wasn't getting anywhere. Now, one would think that I should have been in pain, but not so. My legs just felt sort of numb for a few days and then all of the spines came out on their own. It may be hard to believe, but those thousands of spines did not fester or produce any notable side effects.

Some memories linger on through the years and all it takes is a word or a picture to bring them rushing back. Recently I saw a picture of a lion and a memory came flooding back. During May 2004 I visited a renowned sportsman named Martin Benchoff in Waynesboro, Pennsylvania. Martin had spent a good portion of his

The dead lion. Photo Martin Benchoff.

life hunting big game all around the world, and he had countless trophies, pictures and related stories as proof. One evening we were looking at his photos and I noticed one of a man covered in blood. I asked Martin what had taken place and immediately noticed that his expression changed as the picture brought back a flood of memories.

As the story unfolded I learned that the lion photo held great significance. The hunt, it turned out, was for lions in Africa, and the story certainly grabbed my attention. A guide had set Martin and another hunter in a position close to the carcass a lion had been feeding on. At some point the lion appeared at the carcass and one of the hunters got away a shot that badly wounded the beast. As Martin described it, "You would not believe the speed of the lion's attack unless you were there and witnessed it."

In the blink of an eye the lion covered the distance between them and attacked the guide before anyone could take a shot. In the first few ensuing seconds, the two hunters were unable to shoot for fear of hitting the guide, so they ran to him. Both men fired at point-blank range as the lion was severely mauling the guide. At least one of the shots hit its mark and the lion, in its death bite, bit right through the barrel of the side-by-side rifle/

The guide after the mauling. Photo Martin Benchoff.

shotgun the guide had been carrying. An aircraft was notified immediately and it landed on a nearby small landing strip. The men fashioned a stretcher to carry the guide to the plane, but he told them what they could do with it and walked onto the plane on his own two feet. Martin pointed out that he was impressed with the guide, who had taken a terrible mauling, but he was even more impressed with the ability of the lion to bite through the shotgun barrel with his death grip.

I can certainly relate to the foregoing story as I recall what it was like to have a grizzly come at me at full speed. Believe me, there is no time for panic or error. In the previous case it is a sure bet that the cool-headed response of the hunters saved the guide's life.

⌣⊥

Any number of strange events can and do take place out in the wilderness. A woods wanderer named Craig Forfar faced a rather embarrassing predicament. He was sledding along with his dog team when he ran out of snow. Imagine finding yourself in the middle of nowhere with your sleighs and no snow. He ended up doing the only thing possible—he unhooked the dogs, set them up with packs, left the sleds and continued along on foot.

Craig Forfar sledding without snow. Photo Eddy Forfar.

Craig Forfar on the Spatsizi River. Photo Eddy Forfar.

Craig Forfar certainly merits a book written about his life. He spent countless years working on surveys in northern BC. He also spent years working with Skook Davidson in the Kechika River area. Just recently I learned that Craig was at Skook's ranch when the house caught fire and burnt to the ground. Skook's radio was lost in the fire so it follows that he was unable to summon help. Craig took it upon himself to walk through the mountains to Muncho Lake where arrangements were made to get assistance for Skook. I spoke with a lady who was at Muncho Lake when Craig arrived and she told me that her first impression of him was that here was a well-tanned, muscular man who was handsome beyond words. She added that her first thought was, "Gee, I wish I were single."

Some pictures do not need an explanation, such as the horse standing still with his pack lying on the ground all apart. These are the kinds of incidents that make guides and outfitters wonder if there isn't an easier way to earn a living. Guides have told me that some things are almost impossible to pack. And let's face it, sooner or later guides manage to pack just about everything the human mind can imagine. Guides Hap and Clara Bowden of Quesnel have photos of boats and cookstoves and all manner of things that their horses packed into the mountains.

The pack horse that lost his pack. Photo Eddy Forfar.

Albino squirrel. Photo Elmer Micks.

Hap told me that he thought his horse almost liked carrying the boat, because it kept the rain off him.

People can spend many years wandering the woods looking for that special photo opportunity, often without any luck. On the other hand, one can step out the door and walk into that once-in-a-lifetime opportunity. Such was the case for woodsman Elmer Micks of Terrace, BC. Apparently he noticed a small, white animal moving through the trees and, as luck would have it, it came out and posed for him. I have spent many years wandering the woods and I have never been fortunate enough to see an albino squirrel.

It is no secret that Elmer Micks spent a great many years in the woods. Fortunately for me, he has sent along a lot of information and photographs. Among these was a picture of a Kermode bear. Often called spirit bears, they are in fact just glorified black bears, although they have a limited range and their numbers are such that they must be protected.

While I'm on the subject of bears, perhaps I should mention that among black bears, 136 kilograms (300 pounds) is a respectable size. Only twice have I spotted huge black bears. On the first occasion I didn't realize what I was looking at. Except for the colour, I would have sworn it was a polar bear because it appeared to have a long neck and small front

Kermode or spirit bear. Photo Leif Eide.

shoulders. The other big black bear I saw looked identical to the first, and someone else who observed it thought it was a grizzly bear. The obvious reason for the bear's strange build is that black bears do not dig like grizzlies and therefore do not develop the large shoulder hump and chest muscles. I think each of these bears weighed at least 320 kilograms (700 pounds) and possibly more. Unfortunately I did not have a camera when I ran into these bears, but my friend Steve Marynovich did when he spotted one of these huge beasts from a helicopter. I can readily understand why people mistake these large black bears for grizzlies. They simply look too big to be black bears.

Bears can be a constant threat to vehicles along the highways during the months of May and June. They have just emerged from their dens and are desperately hungry. Due care should be used while driving, especially along roadways where there is an abundance of fresh green grass. While driving at night, we should always be on the lookout for eyes reflecting back at us. This warning can prevent terrible accidents; striking a large bear can do enormous damage to a car. I knew an individual who struck and killed a black bear near Bear Lake and luckily received only minor injuries. When he emerged from the car he said, "It felt like I hit a brick wall."

Grizzlies are strange creatures, generally roaming the woods alone except during mating season or, unfortunately, in garbage dumps or salmon streams where they are known to bunch up in great numbers. Bears love avalanche lilies around the timberline, and while they don't bunch up, there may be many of them in a small area. From my experience, they like to keep at least 50 metres (165 feet) distance between families. I'm positive that they feel a sense of security knowing there are other bears nearby. In these cases it is common to see boar grizzlies completely in the open throughout the day, something we seldom ever saw 40 or 50 years ago. There is a picture floating around of over 40 grizzlies bunched up along the McNeil River in Alaska. These bears seem to understand that they all have a need to be there, although the biggest bears take possession of the best salmon fishing spots.

There is an old wives' tale that boar grizzlies put claw marks as high up in trees as they can reach, and this forces all other bears to stay away. This is absolute nonsense. What has become apparent to us is that when there are an abundance of grizzlies in an area, the black bears generally tend to stay away.

There are so many strange things that occur in nature if a person is lucky enough to observe them. Just this very day I learned that my brother-in-law, Lloyd Vandermark of McBride, witnessed a most unusual sight. He was visiting his brother on a farm in Alberta when he heard a weird commotion going on behind a building where he had just been a moment earlier. He went back to investigate and found two yellow-bellied sapsuckers engaged in a life-and-death fight that went on for at least five minutes. The battle must have started in the sky. Finally one of the birds was injured to the point where it lost consciousness. The winner kept up its vicious attack for several minutes. When it left, Lloyd checked and confirmed that the other bird was indeed dead. He looked around but could not find the third bird that he suspected was the cause of the fight. A truly strange event to witness, Lloyd described it as "the once-in-a-lifetime occurrence that I'll never forget."

Vince's bloodstained clothes.
Photo Vince Vecchio.

Lloyd also told me one of the strangest stories that has ever come my way. He sent along some photos of the rifle involved in this adventure. I pursued the story by interviewing the main party involved, Vince Vecchio of McBride, BC.

This strange incident took place September 16, 2006, when Vince and a friend named Greggo Mutch were hunting for a grizzly bear near Buchanan Creek in the McGregor River watershed. After a bit of dry luck, Vince got a shot away with his .300 Weatherby Magnum at what appeared to be a three- or four-year-old grizzly. At the shot, it appeared the bear had been hit hard, but it managed to take off into the woods. An experienced hunter, Vince knew about the tendency of grizzlies to circle and lie in wait for their pursuer(s), so they waited an hour to let the bear die. Then they went to the spot where the bear had stood when it was struck by the bullet, and it was instantly apparent from the green in the blood trail that it had been gut-shot—a dangerous situation under any circumstances.

They waited a considerable length of time and then Greggo stayed put while Vince made a large circle to intercept the bear's blood trail. When he completed the circle he returned to Greggo with the news that the bear was still somewhere in the thick brush right close to them. Again they waited an hour and then Vince made a much smaller circle. When he completed that circle they realized that the bear was indeed very close at hand and so they assumed it was dead. Suddenly Vince saw a movement in the thick brush, and as it ran off he realized it was the bear and it was still very much alive.

Again they waited for a while and at last realized that they had to act, as the day was wasting away and they didn't want to leave a wounded bear that could possibly kill a passerby. They followed the blood trail; suddenly it turned hard to the right. They adjusted and walked only a few metres when the bear attacked from behind. As so many hunters have learned the hard way, the bear had circled and lain in wait. Vince raised his rifle to shoot, but the bear was on him before he could fire. It knocked him down, and in the process his rifle flew out of his hands.

As the bear pushed him down, Vince got his feet into its gut and, with all his strength, sent it flying about 3 metres (10 feet) away. Before he could look for his rifle, it was back on him again. Vince pulled out his hunting knife and struck the bear in the ribs, but the blade broke. In an effort to protect his vital organs, Vince rolled over; this allowed the bear to viciously attack his head and back. In what must have seemed like eons but was only a minute, the bear put nine puncture holes in his back and chewed up his head and ears. In a last-ditch attempt to get away, Vince rolled down the hill, but the bear was on him again with a bite to his thigh.

Vince knew he had to fight back or he would be killed, so he slugged the bear in the nose with all his might. At that point it backed off, and when it came at him again, Vince drove it in the nose with his elbow. That appeared to be the bear's Achilles heel, so he gave it the elbow-to-the-nose treatment several more times.

During the scuffle, Greggo had been trying to help but was afraid of shooting Vince instead of the bear. Vince had repeatedly shouted to him, "Don't shoot me!" At risk to himself, Greggo came around right beside

Greggo Mutch with grizzly. Photo Vince Vecchio.

Vince and emptied all his bullets into the bear at point-blank range. Of course it was game over for the bear at that point, so the men went about dressing Vince's wounds, which were numerous.

Since Vince was badly hurt, Greggo offered to carry him back to their vehicle but Vince refused. Instead, as soon as they got the bleeding under control, they went to skin the bear and pack it out with them. As they dressed out the bear they solved a mystery: during the fight Vince had pulled his knife and stabbed the bear several times in its ribs; the blade had broken off and they found it inside the carcass. Another surprise awaited them when they rolled the bear over. They discovered Vince's rifle and noticed a most peculiar thing. One of the bullets that Greggo had fired had struck the barrel of Vince's rifle and penetrated halfway through.

Imagine how perfectly the bullet had to strike the barrel so that it would not ricochet. What a day they endured, but unlucky as it was, it could have been worse. Had it been a large bear, it's almost certain that Vince would have been killed. Remember, this bear was still alive and mobile at least two hours after being gut-shot. Grizzlies gut-shot with soft-point expanding bullets die within 15 minutes due to massive hemorrhaging.

The rifle involved in Vince's mauling was a .300 Weatherby Magnum. There are six other cases where bears were wounded by these rifles. Four of the bears escaped wounded and were never found. This probably means that these bears died a slow death somewhere in the woods. My brother Clarence can tell a few stories of that nature; in one case the grizzly was wounded by a .270 and a .300 Weatherby Magnum. The bear got back up and attacked them at full speed. Clarence shot it under the bottom jaw and stopped it at point-blank range. His rifle was a .30-06 with copper-point expanding bullets. In another case one of our hunting partners used this same sort of bullet on a large boar grizzly as it ran away through the woods. The bullet struck the bear in a hind leg and it ran only about 70 metres (230 feet) before it collapsed and died from massive hemorrhaging.

I'm not blaming Weatherby. The problem lies with the bullets that are designed to hold together even if they hit bone. Because of that, they shoot completely through a large animal leaving only a tiny exit hole. As for the gut-shot two-year-old, I want to dwell on it for a moment in the hope that I can prevent another mauling. But in order to do so, I must tell you the following story, which is just one of several similar experiences we have had throughout the years.

About 35 years ago a close friend from Prince George asked me to help him get a grizzly and I agreed. I knew of a perfect spot to take him, the place where a grizzly had dragged a train-killed moose from the railroad grade to the edge of the nearby woods.

Vic Litnosky and I had been friends since childhood, but I had serious reservations about taking him after bear when I learned that he owned a 7mm Weatherby Magnum and was using Nosler-type partition bullets. This was the gun he brought to the fight. Well, we went to the area a couple of hours before dark and got situated in behind a large fallen tree. This was a dream opportunity only 30 metres (100 feet) from the carcass. A strong crosswind prevented the bear from getting our scent, so everything was in our favour. We sat in absolute silence, patiently waiting. After perhaps an hour had passed, and just as the evening hush settled the woods, I heard a twig snap and motioned to Vic that the bear was coming. A moment later a most beautiful brown-coloured grizzly emerged from the shadows and started feasting on the carcass. I nodded to Vic to shoot and he calmly laid his rifle over the tree in what I figured was a sure thing.

I watched the bear closely as Vic fired and I clearly saw hair fly from the neck of the grizzly. Judging from the angle, the bullet had

Grizzly beside Vince. Photo Greggo Mutch.

struck it on the top of the neck only an inch from the spine and went on through the entire chest to emerge somewhere behind the rib cage. In a flash, amid the noise of some mighty roars, the bear rolled head over heels to the bottom of the hill. Then, just as quickly, it regained its feet and was into the woods and gone before we could fire a second shot.

Now came the dirty part. Anyone who has ever trailed a wounded adult grizzly knows what we had to contend with. We followed the bear's blood trail and soon noticed that it headed into the thickest brush around. At the start, the blood drops were almost continuous. No heavy bleeding, because the small exit hole does not allow it, but by the time we covered a few hundred metres, the blood spots were few and far between. What a hair-raising experience that was; I'll bet it took us the better part of an hour to cover a distance of about 300 to 400 metres (1,000 to 1,300 feet). Vic stayed about 10 metres (33 feet) behind me and slightly off to one side as we carefully checked everywhere the bear could have lain in wait; this bear was not going to get us by surprise. Finally we ran out of sign, and the impending darkness gave us no alternative but to abort the chase.

The next morning we returned to the spot where we had stopped the evening before but no sign was found. Obviously the blood had clotted and plugged the hole where the bullet had emerged. Judging by where the bullet had struck the bear, I have no doubt that it was a fatal shot, but heaven only knows how much that bear suffered and how far it may have travelled before it died.

I could go on and on about similar situations and the obvious suffering that goes with it. In another case, Norm Pidherny and I were walking the railroad tracks looking for bears on train-killed moose. The year was 1975 and the place was about 125 kilometres (75 miles) east of Prince George. We knew that two other young hunters were hiding near a moose carcass a couple of kilometres distant from us, so when we heard a couple of shots coming from that direction, we decided to investigate.

About 20 minutes later we arrived at the carcass to find the two men all shook up. They had wounded a grizzly only to have it escape into the woods, leaving a blood trail in its wake. It became instantly apparent to me that the bear had been standing in some willows, which threw the bullet to one side, causing it to miss its target. This meant that the bear could be wounded anywhere.

The two men flatly refused to trail the bear; therefore Norm and I decided to take a crack at tracking it down—a dirty and thankless job. The bear had climbed a

A bald eagle. Photo Steve Schwartz.

steep bank adjacent to the railroad grade, and in its trail we found a piece of bone about the size of a thumb and 15 centimetres (6 inches) long. We felt sure that the bear was terribly wounded so we followed it with great care, expecting a charge if it were unable to escape. We climbed up over a hill about a total distance of 100 metres (330 feet) and the blood trail came to an abrupt end. Once again the rifle was a .300 Weatherby Magnum with partition bullets. However, I do not entirely blame the bullets in this case, because that bear went straight to a muskeg. Because of the swiftness with which the bleeding stopped, I'm certain the bear packed his wound with moss. This is one of three cases that I—and others— have dealt with where bears did this same thing: they arrived at a muskeg and shortly the blood trail came to a complete stop.

I cannot state how strongly I feel about these military-style bullets. Obviously they should not be used on wildlife, as the bullets go right on through a large animal without the massive bleeding that would occur with expanding bullets. A gut-shot bear staying alive for several hours simply says it all. Alternately, we have found that with expanding bullets a gut-shot bear is usually dead in less than 15 minutes. Since we cannot guarantee a perfect shot in conditions where a bullet might ricochet, the next best thing we can and should do is use bullets that put animals out of their suffering as quickly as possible.

One point I must elaborate on: if you are in the process of trailing a wounded grizzly that has been travelling in a straight line and then suddenly changes direction, be on guard, because you may already be inside the trap. Unless there is an obvious reason for it having changed direction, such as a large stream, heavy blow-down or a near-vertical ridge, it might have circled and could be lying in wait to attack you from behind.

Finally, I'll close this chapter by relating a strange occurrence that took place during May 1949, an event that some people may refuse to believe. The people involved were the CNR section crew and their foreman, John Patrick, who were stationed in Penny, BC. As they sat waiting for a train to pass so that they could return home, they watched a dozen crows feeding on a train-killed moose. One of the men took it upon himself to try for one of these birds, so he crept through the woods and got away a fatal shot with his .22 calibre rifle. Instantly the other crows flew up and attacked the guard bird that had been derelict in its duty on top of a tree. Several times they dove at it in mid-air until it crash-landed. Then the birds descended and continued their attack until the guard was killed.

My sister Margaret Humphreys and her friend Dot Sherbey had a similar experience while out for a walk in the town of Barriere, BC. As they strolled along they came upon two crows fighting on the ground. They stopped to watch and immediately another crow dove down from its perch on a power line and joined the fray. The new arrival appeared to join the winner and together they tore the other bird to pieces. The women could see no obvious reason for the attack, but the loser must have done something to raise their ire. Is it fair to assume that crows are intelligent creatures with their own strict rules? It certainly seems so.

7.

IN THE MOUNTAINS

I always seem to have a lot in common with people who climb mountains and wander about the woods. Generally speaking, I find them to be a hardy and self-reliant lot. Some have had interesting and surprising experiences that I readily listen to. Often I'm amazed contrary to what I expect, such as when the bush pilot who flew the North for over 20 years said he never saw a pack of wolves numbering more than seven. I think this surprised me more than if he had said 30.

I find it puzzling to view wolves from the perspective of the experts. What a difference there is in their points of view. Some people cannot describe any action among wolf packs without using the alpha explanation; others look at it in a different light.

The idea of an aggressively dominant "alpha wolf" in gray wolf packs has been discredited by many wolf biologists and researchers. The so-called alphas in packs are merely the breeding animals. According to wolf biologist L. David Mech: "Calling a wolf an alpha is usually no more appropriate than referring to a human parent or a doe deer as an alpha. Any parent is dominant to its young offspring, so alpha adds no information."

The eyes of the wolf. Photo Steve Schwartz.

Another individual who studied Arctic wolves for many years described the use of the term "alpha" in wolf packs as equivalent to saying, "Mom and Dad are in charge of the children in that family."

I find it most interesting that many of these researchers have noted

Four wolves, part of a family of six. Photo Steve Schwartz.

other wolves making decisions for the packs, and the breeding pair—or alphas if you must—going along with them in whatever action follows. This does not surprise me, as there are so many things to do and many decisions to be made, especially in a large pack.

Wolves are noted for having the same mate throughout their lives unless their mate dies. Some sources have stated that even then some wolves do not mate again, although age may have a bearing on that. Another interesting point is that wolves can survive up to 13 years in the wild. Regarding the weight of wolves, I take exception to people who state that they have taken 90- to 140- kilogram (200- to 300-pound) wolves. These people, such as the man in the Northwest Territories who recently claimed his displayed wolf weighed 118 kilograms (260 pounds), appear to be blowing air. I have never believed this, as it takes a good-sized dog to weigh over 50 kilograms (110 pounds). According to Alaska State authorities, such huge wolves do not exist; they say that the largest males weigh up to 52 kilograms (115 pounds).

Some experts state that, aside from communal howls where other packs are warned against trespass, the male howls and the pack responds in order to guide the hunter back home. I have heard males guided back from hunts in this manner countless times, as I'm sure many others have. It is a sound that travels great distances, which surely must be necessary when the wolves are separated by distance and ridges. My brother Clarence had a golden opportunity to watch a small wolf pack from an island in the Fraser River. The wolves had taken up residence on the shore of the river where a family of four would stay while the male was out hunting. The wolves howled back and forth until the male returned. In one case it brought back a small rodent, not nearly enough to feed the family. To make matters worse, the male responsible for gathering food had a severe limp, having been injured in some manner. A few months later the family disappeared, possibly the victims of starvation. Certainly that injured male could not be expected to supply sufficient sustenance for the entire family.

One may wonder about the reason for extra-large wolf packs, but one purpose that can be served is that a large pack of wolves, let's say 30, can devour at least 250 kilograms (550 pounds) of flesh at a feeding. This means that an average-sized moose can be cleaned up at one feeding. When we consider that the flesh freezes rock-hard in sub-zero temperatures, the advantage of cleaning it up at one feeding becomes obvious.

Alaska State officials also say that a pack of wolves can have a range of from 780 to 2,600 square kilometres (300 to 1,000 square miles). Obviously the size of the area is dependent upon the size of the packs and the availability of game in the selected areas. Those same officials state that pack size can go beyond 30, a fact that was much more common 60 years ago. I think it's stretching things to a ridiculous end to classify the wolves that follow large herds of caribou as packs. For instance, if 125 wolves are following a herd of 2,000 caribou, they should not be classed as a pack.

Many people refuse to accept the fact that wolves attack humans, despite overwhelming proof. Regardless of one's point of view, wolves are most certainly intriguing and intelligent animals. The number of horses lost to wolves in the Kechika Valley has been disputed, but there is little doubt that it was high. Skook Davidson lost 18 horses to wolves during a winter in the early 1940s, although it may well have happened during a tough winter of unusually deep snowfall when the horses were in poor health.

In an effort to combat the wolf menace, drastic steps were taken. Strychnine was used and enormous numbers of wolves were killed, yet to the surprise of wilderness guides, they kept on moving in from other areas.

Some of the trappers I interviewed years ago said they had found proof of wolves having killed and eaten their own young during periods of starvation. I understand that the breeding animals must survive and that new pups can be produced later, but I'm not entirely convinced that the wolves killed their own young. Perhaps the pups starved to death first and then were eaten by the adults. Somehow it seems to me that it goes against nature for them to kill their own young. I know that mink are noted for killing their own young when stressed, but that is a different situation entirely. Who knows? Perhaps someday a researcher will catch starving wolves in the act of killing their offspring and I will have to eat crow.

Steve Schwartz of Prince George has taken close-up photographs of wildlife for many years, even managing to get close-range pictures of wolves. But a rather strange occurrence took place when he was able to stand just a short distance from some wolves and talk to them. They were lying down when he first spoke to them so they rose and watched him for a few minutes, but Steve was more than a bit surprised when they stretched out for another nap and paid him no attention. Eventually Steve became serious about his shouting and got them to move along. This pack consisted of a mother and five pups. A large adult wolf had been shot in that general area just a few months earlier and Steve believes it was the papa. Again the question arises: are wild animals losing their wildness?

A noted woodsman and river traveller named George Myers had a rather unusual experience with wolves back in the 1930s. He was travelling with his dog team when he stumbled upon a pack of eight wolves at close range. Dogs, wolves and man stood motionless for a minute as they closely studied each other. Finally George started pulling his rifle out of its scabbard and in the blink of an eye the wolves melted into the surrounding woods. Is it any wonder that some woodsmen express the belief that wolves are able to sense our intent?

Ago Bjorklund and Ole Hanson experienced a similar event in the 1930s along the McGregor River. They were following their trapline when a large pack of wolves surrounded them and followed them for 5 kilometres (3 miles), all the way to their main cabin. Throughout the entire trip the wolves howled continually. Ago told me that he could feel his spine tingling right down to his heels, and added that it was the only time that he was really frightened in the woods. When the two men reached the cabin where their rifles were kept, they calmly went in, grabbed their firearms and went back out, only to find that the wolves had all vanished. This left them seriously puzzled as the wolves had walked openly quite close to them along the trail and showed no fear whatsoever. Explain that.

IN THE MOUNTAINS 147

During the 1950s I lived in Grasmere near the Montana border, where deer were abundant. Sometimes I used to sit motionless if I noticed deer approaching. This would cause them to stop and repeatedly stamp the ground with their front feet, obviously trying to get me to move so they could figure out what I was. As with many other animals, deer are curious to a fault.

Ann and Kelly with cougar kittens.

In 1966 I, along with my wife, Ann, and my son, Kelly, visited a long-time friend named Roy Sinclair who lived in Grasmere. During our visit we spent some time with Roy's cousin Bob Totten, who had several cougar hounds and was an accomplished hunter. Just as we arrived in the area, Bob shot a cougar right in his yard. What he didn't know at the time was that the cougar had kittens, and their mama had driven them up a tree right beside his house. Well, Bob captured the kittens and we got a close-up view of their rather unusual personalities. The first thing Bob did after he captured them was to cut off their claws so they could not climb trees. What a funny performance we witnessed as the kittens repeatedly attempted to climb. They would get up a few feet and then slide down, look at their paws and look at the trees. Again and again they repeated this action. It took quite some time before they accepted that they could no longer climb trees. A few days later a conservation officer came by and took them away.

Cougars are among the most curious of animals. Often we are unaware that they are watching us because they can hide so well. Photographer Steve Schwartz has a picture of a cougar taken at a distance of only 30

Mother cougar at close range. Photo Steve Schwartz.

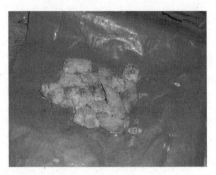

Piles of scat in an abandoned house.
Photo David Humphreys.

metres (100 feet). An avid nature photographer, Steve walked right near the beast and then stood still as it watched him with keen interest. A few minutes passed and then a cougar kitten appeared nearby. Neither cat nor kitten seemed the least bit concerned about their safety and slowly sauntered away into the surrounding woods.

Throughout the years I have heard several stories of cougars spending time in buildings. Recently my nephew David Humphreys showed me some pictures he had taken inside an abandoned house near Likely, BC. There are several different-sized piles of scat lying about the floor and I'm prepared to bet that they are from a family of cougars. What other animals leave piles of scat 3 centimetres (1.2 inches) in diameter? The droppings appear to contain deer hair. When considering the possibility of bears leaving the scat, I don't know of any cases where they stay around a place. From my experience, bears break in and do their thing and then leave. In this case the scat appears to have been left over an extended period of time.

Wildlife can be elusive beyond belief, and there is no more glowing example of that than the fisher, a member of the weasel family. Some people, such as trapper Ernest Jensen, call them "ghosts of the woods," and ghosts are what I think they can be. Some woodsmen have travelled the mountains for 40 or 50 years without getting a glimpse of one, partly because they are nocturnal, and partly because they can be so elusive. For those who have sighted them, a fleeting glimpse is about all they get. It is fun to watch two squirrels chasing each other around a tree in the spring. Often one would swear there are three or four squirrels rather than just two. Realizing that martins can easily catch these squirrels, now go a step further and picture a fisher catching a martin. It then becomes even easier to appreciate the speed of fishers. Elusive as they are, some trappers have outsmarted fishers by imitating rodents in agony.

It is small wonder that I feel the way I do when I state that in all the years I spent glassing game in the mountains I never got so much as a glimpse of a fisher. The two I did manage to see were both spotted while I was driving at night. By comparison, as elusive as cougars are, I have seen a total of six: two kittens that were taken to a zoo, two adults in the mountains, one adult right inside the community of Penny, and one while I was driving the Bowron Road with a fisherman friend, Henry Michalchuk.

⌣

Perhaps the strangest pictures among Steve Schwartz's collection are some he managed to get of foam in the shape of a cone 1.5 metres (5 feet) in height. He suspected it came about when water was running through willows over the top of a beaver dam and the temperature dropped to -23°C (-5°F); a strong north wind added to the chill. A cone of ice quickly built up in the overflow, which in turn filled up with foam. When the ice melted, the foam cone stayed for about another two days before it dissipated. Steve admits that he is just guessing about the origin of the cone, but at the same time he has been offered no other possible explanation.

In all my years in the wilds I have never seen anything to compare with this cone. I sent a picture of the cone to a biologist who says that he has never seen or heard of anything like it and doubts that it occurred the way Steve described it. What makes it so difficult to explain is that the cone rises about 1 metre (3.3 feet) higher than the surrounding terrain.

Steve has managed to get many photos of black and brown bears eating clover in his fields during their courtship adventures. But he told me that he has never found any grizzly tracks around his place; yet he lives in a remote area. Upon studying his pictures I quickly pointed out some grizzlies. Steve was quite surprised and upon closer examination agreed that they were in fact grizzly bears, sometimes in the process of mating. His fields are loaded with clover and it is

Foam cone near a beaver dam. Photo Steve Schwartz.

A black and a brown bear during mating season. Photo Steve Schwartz.

no secret that bears and clover go hand in hand. Another crop with great appeal to bears is oats. They not only like to devour oat crops; they also like to roll around in them and destroy a good portion of what they don't eat. Often the bears will lie down and hide as they eat, so people may be unaware of their presence in oat fields until much damage is done.

Several years after I started roaming the ridges, I found myself wanting to study mountain goats. The rugged and spectacular mountains they frequented were more than enough to hold my interest. In fact, I have had hunters tell me that one of the main reasons they hunted goats and sheep was not to get them as trophies, but to visit the magnificent mountain terrain where they live.

It is small wonder that some goats perish when we consider the almost sheer cliffs they traverse. On a trip into the mountains east of McBride, BC, two friends and I were following a stream, which was named Beaver Creek at that time. As we walked along below a cliff, we spotted a young goat hanging over some limbs in a huge fir tree. It was obvious that it had fallen off the cliff, probably in a snowslide.

Sometimes a person sees sights in the mountains so precious that they would pay big bucks to have a camera in hand, such as the naturalist who was studying goats on a mountain at Trail, BC, when he noticed a black bear sneaking toward a kid. Just as the bear was about to attack, the nanny lowered her head and struck the bear a terrific blow, which sent it rolling down the slope. Without looking back, the bear continued on its way, probably in search of an easier victim.

It was during the summer of 1991 when I took my daughter, Kim, and her friend Tara Harrison on a trip through the parks between Jasper and Banff, Alberta. When we came upon a small herd of goats on the highway, the girls

Mountain goat runs across a cliff. Photo Wilf Moore.

asked me to pull over so they could get out and watch the animals. I was on one side of my truck and the girls were on the other when suddenly a horrible scream erupted. In the excitement, Kim had locked her door, which prevented Tara from gaining access to the vehicle. With no other

The mama goat that attacked Tara.

option Tara came streaking around the vehicle with mama goat right behind her. I quickly jumped out and drew the goat's attention, which gave Tara time to get back into the truck.

As soon as things quieted down I quizzed Tara about what had happened. In between panic-stricken gasps for breath, she admitted she had been trying to pet the kid when its mama attacked her. I asked her if she would have tried to pet a bear cub, if that's what had been by the road. Her answer: "Sure, they're cute!"

I was alarmed to learn that no one had ever warned this teenager about the danger of wild animals with young. How is it possible that a child can go through years of schooling and not be aware of this? I think that we have far too many Walt Disney-type shows on television, and many of our young people have no perception of the reality of nature. As well, there are far too many videos of people feeding and playing with wildlife that has been tamed. Children lack the ability to discern the difference between what is staged and what is real. If a child repeatedly sees people playing with wildlife, why wouldn't they believe it? There should be a responsibility on the part of wildlife experts to spend a bit of time in classrooms separating fact from fiction for our children, since the parents often fail to do so.

Twenty miles of grassland. Photo Eddy Forfar.

John Gaspery hauling moose. Photo Arne Mellows.

It is common knowledge that bears and wolves prey on moose calves. On one occasion I saw two coyotes following a moose with two calves. Naturally I assumed they were trying to cripple one of the calves. Their method is quite simple: they bide their time until they can catch one of the calves by surprise and then they attack. They have only to seriously injure a calf and then wait. Sooner or later the mother moose will have to leave the injured calf and then the attack begins. David Wlasitz of Prince George saw a small black bear attempting to get a calf, but the mother sensed the bear's intent and, in a flash, chased it away.

A century ago it was common practice to ford streams and even rivers with horses; often it was the only means of moving supplies to remote areas. The accompanying photo shows how a moose was moved down Slim Creek. There were simply no other means available as no one was about to carry the moose a distance of 15 kilometres (9 miles). John Gaspery of Dome Creek put his horses to the test and succeeded where many other folks would have flatly refused to try. There is no doubt that even a stumble would have meant a tragic end for both animals. Horses harnessed together are unable to swim, and death is certain if they go down.

People sometimes wonder about the abundance of horses years ago. "Where did they get food for them?" has been an oft-asked question. I have wondered myself when I walked through miles of thick timber. The proper people to ask are pack train operators. They found meadows spread here and there throughout the woods, even fairly high up in the mountains. In places there was grassland that spread for miles on end where horses managed to paw up sufficient browse to survive the winters, and still do. Windswept ridges are required, and places like the Kechika Valley are capable of wintering hundreds of horses, providing they can elude the wolf packs.

⟶⟵

Since this chapter is about the mountains, perhaps I should point out a few helpful tricks and hints for personal safety. Some are quite simple, such as using cardboard under our sleeping bags to prevent cold attacking us from below. It is almost weightless and easy to carry, but it must be kept dry to be effective.

A prospector told me another trick that saved at least one life. He was surprised by an early, heavy snowstorm while he was quite some distance from his camp. Somehow he had either lost or misplaced his

Pack train crossing talus slope. Photo Eddy Forfar.

lighter so he was unable to get a fire going for warmth. He had left his snowshoes at his tent and so he had to fight his way through the snow, but he played out about halfway back to camp just as darkness overtook him. Forced to spend a night out in the elements, he dug down into a bed of cones that had piled up under an old fir tree. He survived the night in relative warmth while the snowstorm raged around him. The next day he returned to his tent, none the worse for what could have been a disastrous bout with hypothermia.

Almost anything can act as insulation in a pinch. Four men who were trapped in trees in Williston Lake for two days and nights after their boat sank took a rather innovative approach. They wisely used the only thing available; they tore an abundance of leaves off the surrounding trees and stuffed them inside their clothing. It worked and was instrumental in saving their lives during the two nights they spent hanging in trees. In a similar manner, dried moss can act as insulation and makes a marvellous bed. Back when I was a lad it was common to find a 10- to 15- centimetre (4- to 6-inch) layer of boughs or moss in the bunks of trappers' cabins. Likewise spruce boughs were used in pits dug down an arm's length under the cabin floors to preserve apples and oranges, sometimes for up to two months, weather permitting.

I have lost track of the number of times that I found caribou resting on snowfields during the heat of summer. They will bed down in the middle of a snowfield so they have a good view in all directions; this lessens the chance of a predator getting them. Besides going there to cool off, they also find relief from the flies that can drive wildlife absolutely crazy during the summer months. Often grizzly bears will dig into the packed snow right beside a rock cliff. I have seen bears playing in the open on snowfields but I have never found them bedded down there. I firmly believe they are smart enough to know that they are too conspicuous out on the open snow; therefore they bed down against a cliff or rock face right at the edge of the snowfield.

I have also seen a mother grizzly bring her cubs out of a tunnel that water had formed in the ice of a snowfield. Imagine the position people would be in if they entered a spot like that when the grizzlies were in there.

There is no substitute for a good pair of binoculars when one is travelling high in the mountains in good grizzly country. We used to frequently glass the area ahead of our direction of travel. I'm sure that on

Four grizzlies eating grass. Photo Paul Paulson.

more than one occasion we prevented a bad situation from occurring by spotting the bears before we moved into an area.

When I sit and reminisce about all the years I have studied bears, I try to come up with some conclusions. Such as, how many grizzlies are there in an average family? I'm sure that it has averaged over two, as I have seen more mamas with three cubs than with one. I have to add a rider to that statement though, because I believe that mothers have more cubs now than they did 40 or 50 years ago when I seldom saw more than two cubs. The reason? I believe there is far more food available now because of logging. The endless cutblocks contain a harvest of plants and berries that were not available in the solid stands of timber that prevailed before 1950. The exceptions, of course, were areas burnt off by forest fires, and it is no secret that the animals congregated there in droves.

8.

WILD WATER

People who love wilderness adventure should thoroughly enjoy the following story. It first came to my attention when I met Pamela and Geoff MacDonald in 2008. These two adventurers had already made their trip from Oak Bay at Victoria to the Grand Canyon of the Fraser River. With them was their travelling companion, a huge husky dog named Taq, without doubt one of the most beautiful dogs I have ever laid eyes on. The purpose of their trip and their adventures to date are told here in their own words:

> Our journey began in Victoria, BC; our planned destination: St. John's, Newfoundland. We felt that the research and planning that could reasonably be done by two people who planned to traverse a landscape and topography as varied as Canada was complete. Two principles guided us: we could adapt, and would to whatever we had to; and we had time enough to be patient, avoiding unnecessary risks.
>
> Most Cross-Canada canoe travellers venture from east to west, ending with a descent down Mackenzie's river. Not us. We decided early on that we were going to travel from capitol to capitol (Victoria to St. John's) and that we should get the "hard" part (BC) over with first. It also occurred to us that in order to satisfy our quest to experience as many Canadian landscapes as possible, we'd have to experience BC's coast.

Author flanked by Pamela and Geoff MacDonald.

And so, on March 22, 2007, we left Oak Bay at Victoria. Our learning curve was steep. We faced numerous storms that set us back by days because an open canoe (we did have a spray deck with a dog sticking out) is unforgiving in rough seas. We calibrated our courage with the marine conditions as broadcast via VHF radio from the various lighthouses along the coast. Our maximums were 1-metre (3-foot) moderate seas and 15-knot winds.

Both of us grew up inland. We had never lived with the tides or the sea. We respected the fact that the ocean had currents, and felt that we had a good basis to venture forth: after all, we'd run hundreds of rapids on rivers before, and we'd paddled the Great Lakes a few times too. We were still surprised, however, when we had our first hair-raising experience. We exited Discovery Passage and turned westward into Johnstone Strait. We blew past Chatham Point lighthouse with tailwind and current aligned, at a record 7 knots with our sail up, catching our breath along the north shore in the protected lee of the Walkem Islands.

As we continued westward, the ebbing tide was ripping from Mayne Passage as we crossed it, and the south wind was generating massive turbulence against the Knox Hill cliffs. It is hard to describe the wild seas that resulted, but the massive stump of a tree, which dwarfed our 5.5-metre (18-foot) canoe, was being thrown around in the current and waves without mercy. Forced to brace with every stroke, only our sail afforded us the ability to continue faster than the current so that we could steer. When we passed Needham Point we could see into Knox Bay, a one-mile-square bay that at the moment was completely occupied by the largest eddy either of us had ever seen. Unbelievable! We fought to access the eddy, and while we caught our breath we circulated until we realized that we would soon be thrown back into the mayhem. We raced to shore only to find fresh bear sign, but we felt that was the lesser of two dangers and camped for three days to regain our nerve and face the hostile Johnstone Strait again.

Good weather days saw us travel more than 56 kilometres (30 nautical miles), but many days we were forced to camp before 10 a.m. when the wind would blow up. On average we travelled about 28 kilometres (15 nautical miles) each day. We only experienced ocean swell from Queen Charlotte Strait until we entered Fitz Hugh Sound. This stretch required only two paddling days for us (although it required several more to wait out the bad weather in between). After camping on a beautiful sand beach for about five days to await good weather, we had the fortune of rounding Cape Caution without incident on a calm and smooth day. We paddled more than 56 kilometres (30 nautical miles)—a record distance for one day.

While camped at Fury Island, we learned that our planned portage route across the Coast Range at Kimsquit was impassable. That route required an 18-kilometre (11-mile) traverse of a logging road that had unfortunately, and unbeknownst to us, been decommissioned several years ago. To make matters worse, the pass we planned to traverse after we left the road had accumulated a record snowpack over the winter. We had expected a gruelling Coast Range portage since the trip's inception, but these two factors meant that this portage would take more than two weeks, a week more than we had anticipated. This led us to consider our alternate plan—a traverse of the pass at Kemano, near Kitimat. We called friends and family to make the necessary arrangements for maps and gear to be sent to Kitimat instead of Bella Coola, where we would resupply.

At Shearwater/Bella Bella we enjoyed much-deserved showers and resupplied with some staples before returning to the sea and making our way north to Kitimat. From Bella Bella the Seaforth Channel leads, as its name suggests, to the open ocean. Swell reappeared as we rounded the reefs associated with Harmston Island. Unfortunately two large cruise ships passed at this point, their wakes building with the swell and rising chop to create intense conditions around the reefs. We braced hard and struggled for a few minutes until we could access Passage Cove. A ripping ebb tide greeted us at Perceval Narrows, but we managed to climb the ebbing tide here and make our way into Mathieson Channel.

We chose Griffin Passage to access Finlayson Channel. Near its entrance we were greeted by a particularly rough tidal rapid (class 3) where we waited a couple of hours for the tide to ebb and turn. It slowed but never turned, and we continued the entire passage bucking it. Two days later we would learn of a kayaker who paddled through Griffin Passage the same direction as us, the tide with him the whole way. Such is life with the tides, their regional trend evident, but their local character unpredictable.

We camped that night with a clear view of the Carter Bay shipwreck emergent from the shallow water — a monument to a heroic captain who ran aground at sea and managed to get his vessel into the shallow bay in time to save all aboard. After Butedale, where we weren't fortunate to witness the Kermode bear who frequents the beach there, we continued to Bishop Bay Hot Springs where we soaked and were subsequently invited aboard an Alaska-bound yacht for the night. Aboard the *Nexus* we were treated to southern hospitality complete with buttered steak and red wine. We spent a dry night in the pilothouse and then made our way up the Boxer Reach of Ursula Channel. Its magnificent impression is forever burned into our memories: one of the BC coast's most awe-inspiring reaches. Two days later, and another soak in a natural hot spring at Weewanie, we arrived in Kitimat.

We spent several days there, resupplying our provisions and making trips to the Greyhound station to send home our ocean equipment and collect the continental equipment we would require for the next leg of our trip. Only 111 kilometres (60 miles) of saltwater remained (until the Atlantic of course), but the Pacific wasn't to give up easily. We took the Gardner Canal, a fiord-like channel buttressed by 2,000-metre (6,600-foot) glaciated peaks, to Kemano. This would be our starting point for our Coast Mountain portage. Although the level of the Gardner Canal in spring fluctuates with the tides, the cooler fresh water cascading from the surrounding peaks constantly flows seaward: unless you are at shore and can see the water level rising, there is no apparent "flood tide" in the Gardner Canal in June. The lighter fresh water, which floats on the surface, always flows oceanward. During ebb that flow exceeds 4 knots, which would hold us in place until the tides turned. We hugged shore closely and at times were treated to fast eddies that countered the overall current. Fortunately we had two natural hot springs to recover at in the evenings.

We said our goodbye to the saltwater at Kemano Beach, loaded our canoe onto a cart and harnessed

Grizzly scat was everywhere. Photo courtesy the MacDonalds.

the three of us. The first 10 kilometres (6 miles) of the portage followed the road to the power station, Alcan's generating station for the aluminum smelter at Kitimat. Although power plant workers advised us that they had seen as many as 29 grizzly bears along the 10-kilometre (6-mile) stretch of pavement leading to the power station, we were fortunate to see only a sow and two cubs, and a boar who lingered at the bowling alley, inside which Alcan staff kindly allowed us to camp.

We toured the power station, which harnesses the energy of diverted water from the Nechako watershed, tunnelled through the Coast Range for 10 kilometres (6 miles) before falling 800 metres (2,640 feet) to the turbines at Kemano. The power station is colossal, and we were duly impressed by it and the warm hospitality afforded us by its staff.

After a hot, greasy breakfast, the staff used a pickup to chase off the resident boar grizzly, and we were on our way up the second leg of the portage. We portaged

30 kilometres (18 miles) along Seekwyakin Creek, using an abandoned jeep road, which until 2000 was used to access the turbine intakes at Tahtsa Lake. Since its abandonment, several creeks which cross the steep-sided road have slid, forcing us to make portages within the portage—unloading the canoe and carrying everything the length of the washout.

Our plan on this day was to reach the snow line where our risk of encountering grizzly bears throughout the night would be reduced. We had a strong motivation—there was grizzly dung at least every 3 metres (10 feet) the entire length of the trail. Our voices were hoarse—we hollered every time we passed a dung pile. Unfortunately, we didn't reach the snow line and were forced to spend an anxious night camped on the trail between piles of grizzly scat. Thankfully, we didn't encounter any bears that night, and the next morning we slogged through to the snow line. From there we reloaded all of our gear into the canoe and dragged it, as if it were a sled, the rest of the way to the Nechako reservoir at Tahtsa Lake.

Crossing a snow bridge during Kemano portage. Photo courtesy the MacDonalds.

Geoff pulling porcupine quills from Taq's nose. Photo courtesy the MacDonalds.

What we did not need, after a gruelling day's hike, was Taq running to us with his nose full of porcupine quills. He was continually rubbing his face in the snow in a futile effort to remove them. He was exceptionally patient while we removed them, except for the quills inside his nose. Geoff had to hold him down while I pulled them out with a Leatherman.

Tahtsa Lake is the westernmost reach of the Nechako reservoir. The record snowpack of that winter resulted in the 200-kilometre (122-mile) long reservoir being at capacity, and that meant that the spillway at Skins Lake was discharging water at rates never before recorded into the Nechako River. In fact, the previous record was being doubled, and it remained that way until September.

We were rapidly approaching Cheslatta Falls. The access to the portage was choked with flooded timber and debris from the beetle-infested pine forest. Accessing the portage was treacherous; missing it would have meant certain death in the engorged falls below. Would the entire reach of the river be like this? What should have been swift water, possibly a class 1 rapid, below the falls was a certain class 3. All research into the river character was moot; the Nechako River had never handled this amount of flow since the construction of the reservoir 50 years ago. After due consideration, we decided to abort the trip until the water levels receded.

After an absence of two months, we returned and continued with the trip. The Nechako River's fury with the melting snow had abated, and we cruised its length to Prince George in a few days. Isle de Pierre was the only significant rapid we faced, and a side channel made it an easy run.

At Prince George we turned left. Right would have taken us downstream and back to the Pacific Ocean. Left was up Fraser's mighty river. It was fall and the glaciers which feed the Fraser had long stopped melting, the resulting low water made our chances of successfully climbing this watershed possible. We expected to make 10 kilometres (6 miles) each day, and if we could manage that, the 520 kilometres (317 miles) to Tête Jaune

Finally on the Nechako River. Photo courtesy the MacDonalds.

Cache on the upper river would gradually pass. We knew we couldn't manage it all this season, but we could get a good start and return in April as soon as the ice melted.

We had calculated correctly, except that it took us a few days to realize this. The river below Giscome Rapids is fast and turbulent, and some days we only managed 3 kilometres (2 miles). At that rate we didn't think we would ever ascend the river and decided that at the Giscome Portage we would traverse to the Peace River. But as time went on, and we reached the crest of the Giscome Rapids, our daily progress increased significantly. With the success we grew to love the river—the love one feels toward a game like chess. You have to be strategic; you have to plan every step of the journey. You have to use every eddy and oxbow to your advantage. And when you realize that by doing this you can make upstream progress, you find yourself in a relationship with a river that you didn't expect.

Tracking the canoe on the Fraser River. Photo courtesy the MacDonalds.

We took advantage of the fact that the current is significantly slower on the inside bend of a river. We tracked the canoe this way on hundreds of bends along the Fraser River. Once around a bend, we would get in the canoe and paddle across to the inside of the next bend. This action saved us an enormous amount of hard work.

We received a lot of help from the people we met in the old mill towns; they told us of friends in the next town and so on and so forth. At each town along the way we had a welcoming committee. The people of the Fraser are wonderful. One stretch gave us pause. Many people went out of their way to warn us about it and the lives it had taken. It snowed as we entered the Grand Canyon of the Fraser; the setting was serene and foreboding. We could hear the mighty waters churning above, but as we inched our way from eddy to eddy, turn to turn, we found our way to the final ledges of the lower canyon. At any higher water level we would never have made it this far. It was worth a try to attempt the last ledges by hard paddling. We scouted it diligently and then made our way across by inching our way against the driving current. Whirlpools appeared, several feet across. The river was far too strong; in fact, Geoff was paddling so hard he broke his paddle. We retreated and carried our canoe and gear above this set of rapids.

Between the two canyons lies Cannibal Bar, reputed to have been the final resting place of men who were trapped on the bar and, through starvation, turned to cannibalism. We camped on shore across from it at the base of the upper canyon. There was no option to paddle our way up any part of this canyon, and so we cleared our way through the portage. We were wet; snow blanketed the area. At the end we felled a small dead fir and dried our wet clothes around its warm glow. The most treacherous part of our journey up the Fraser was over.

The MacDonalds had to stop because several inches of snow told them winter had arrived. A friend came from Alberta to get them and their gear. The next April they resumed their cross-Canada trip after the river shed its coat of ice. Their story continues:

> We returned the following April and waited for the ice to break up so that we could set out again. We encountered a cow moose on the first gravel bar we planned to camp on—apparently it was a good calving ground. We would have moved on, but she left first. Tracking up the icy banks, and paddling across the oxbows, we made steady progress beyond Goat River Rapids, McBride and Dunster. But the river was rising, and by now it was rising more than a foot each night. Camping was tricky, especially after warm days. We would remind ourselves that it was runoff time as we looked to the snowpacked mountains melting above.
>
> Six weeks of paddling since we started at Prince George and we arrived at Tête Jaune. We had managed to average 10 kilometres (6 miles) per day (including rest days), and we celebrated our triumph. Another 35 kilometres (21 miles) of portaging led us to Kinbasket Lake and the Columbia River. Kinbasket Lake is a reservoir 200 kilometres (122 miles) in length, its outfall at the Mica Dam. Kinbasket is a contradiction; it is flanked by glaciers—the Rockies, Monashees and Selkirks. But it is remote and it is a man-made artifact, and so it has been heavily logged. The glaciers that flank it provide katabatic and anabatic [downward- and upward-flowing] winds. In places five valleys converge at the lake. Wind direction can be unpredictable but severe, and the long reaches provide ample opportunity for significant chop to arise. We were lucky; we paddled the length of the lake in a week, with only one windy day.
>
> We portaged Red Grave Canyon on the Columbia and then fought our way the rest of the way up the Columbia to Golden. Meltwater-swollen, the Columbia

Descending a ridge in Wolverine Pass. Photo courtesy the MacDonalds.

was very challenging. Driftwood clogged the heads of the bars, and the braided nature of the river meant that following oxbows was not an option. There were a few tense moments where we were only making inches of progress despite paddling at top speed. Eventually we reached the Kicking Horse River, and after two tries we crossed it and entered the Columbia marsh—a birder's paradise.

We made our way leisurely up the Columbia from there to Harrogate. At Harrogate we took our gear out of the water again and started another heinous leg of our cross-Canada journey. The reward was great—after this portage we would follow the current downstream for 2,000 kilometres (1,222 miles) across the prairies. But first we had three mountain passes and 100 kilometres (60 miles) of portaging to finish.

The first pass had been seldom used, so we had to clear the trail for the first 1,400 vertical metres (4,620 feet). This took about five days; we then dropped down

Ball Pass on the Continental Divide. Photo courtesy the MacDonalds.

into the Beaverfoot Valley before climbing up to Wolverine Pass in Kootenay National Park. We were among the first that year, except for a large grizzly that had traversed the pass just before us. We descended to Numa Creek and then climbed Ball Pass via Hawk Creek before descending to the Bow River at Red Earth Creek. At Ball Pass we drank champagne. The first and most challenging province was behind us; even more exciting was the prospect of paddling with the current instead of against it.

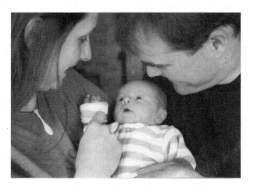

Pam, Geoff and Jude MacDonald. Photo courtesy the MacDonalds.

Two weeks after we left the Columbia, we were back in the water, on the other side of the Continental Divide. Warm prairie summer weather baked us as we cruised, some days managing more than 70 kilometres (42 miles) across Alberta and Saskatchewan.

At the time of writing this we are headed to Cumberland House, SK, to begin our third season of paddling. Jude, our eight-and-a-half-month-old son, will be joining us this season.

From Cumberland House we will paddle around Lake Winnipeg and up the Bloodvein River into Ontario. The Albany River will lead us eastward toward James Bay, but prior to reaching it we plan to cross another watershed and enter Lake Superior, making our way eastward into Lake Huron, up the French River and into Quebec. Our final destination is St. John's, NL. Our route will evolve as we approach the east coast.

I surely envy the MacDonalds; what a fantastic adventure they have undertaken. Jude may be too young to remember, but I think he will become the youngest canoeist to travel halfway across Canada. I also feel certain the baby is in good hands, as the parents have experienced virtually every type of water situation and will take no chances. For those who care to follow their journey, please take note: the message across both sides of their canoe can be seen from a distance. It proclaims CANOE-ACROSSCANADA.CA.

As with others who have experienced adventurous undertakings, I feel sure their memories will last a lifetime.

⌣

During the past century an enormous change has taken place in water transport. One hundred years ago people were using rafts, scows and primitive dugout canoes to travel our waterways. Without floatation devices they were sitting ducks for tragedy.

Slowly this changed as better and better boats were designed. Then along came outboard motors and eventually jet boats as more and more the wild water was challenged and conquered. Although some of the people who got involved with jet boats years ago have travelled many of our rivers, I'll bet that few have as many hours on the rivers as Ben Meisner of Prince George. Ben cannot say enough about Gordon Ford, who was involved in racing in New Zealand before coming to Canada. The original owner of Ali-Craft Boats in Prince George, he built some of the first boats for Ben. In an effort to determine just how many of our rivers Ben has run, I soon realized it would be much simpler to list the rivers he did not run, as they are in the minority. Ben lived in Kamloops for a time and was active on the North Thompson River when people used to float it on wooden rafts. This is a fast river with many logjams, and people soon realized it was too dangerous for that type of rafting. In total, Ben assisted in pulling nine people from its waters. The last year these rafts were used, two people were drowned.

Sometimes a person happens to be in the right place at the right time to luck out and find an explanation for something that has puzzled them for many years. Case in point, Ben Meisner was travelling the McGregor River when he spotted a grizzly burying a moose carcass along the riverbank. He carried on with his journey, and when he returned sometime later he found a wolverine on the same carcass. About 400

Ben in Mud River Rapids, 1993. Photo Ben Meisner.

metres (1,300 feet) downriver he saw the same grizzly wandering along. Ben put the two together and came up with an explanation for a thing that had puzzled me for many years—why do grizzlies bury carcasses and never dig them up again? The obvious answer is that a wolverine has sprayed the carcass and neither the bear nor any other woodland creature will touch it after that. Ben and his companion stopped to investigate and found that the wolverine had indeed sprayed the carcass, and the stink was unbearable. I had heard this same thing from several guides and trappers but had never proved it for myself.

This explains why I have found carcasses buried by grizzlies that never returned to the carcass to eat. They probably had returned to the carcass, took a sniff and left in disgust. Ben was extremely lucky to actually witness it happening.

Some of Ben's experiences were hard to classify. I mean it was hard to determine whether they were humorous or tragic, such as the time he went up the Torpy River with a local doctor, each in his own boat. The salmon must have been in the river at the time, because in that one run along the river they saw five grizzlies, and some were very close to their boats. Prior to the trip, Ben questioned the good doctor if he had sufficient gas to make the trip and was assured he did. Well, they were cruising peacefully along about 55 kilometres (33 miles) up the river when the doctor's boat stopped, and you guessed it—he had run out of gas. Ben had no alternative but to return downriver to Walker Creek where his vehicle was parked. Then he had to drive to McBride and return with a load of fuel. This was a 180-kilometre (110-mile) trip in itself. Back at Walker Creek, he still had to travel 55 kilometres (33 miles) upriver to rescue his friend. So much for good planning.

A memory that will never die leapt into Ben's mind as he told me about the time he was heading up the Stikine River through an area with several lattices or channels, if you prefer. He glanced to the side and thought he saw a person sitting on a sweep near the shore. He felt so certain about what he had glimpsed that he turned the boat and went back downriver. Sure enough, a woman was hanging on to a sweep (a tree that sticks out into the river) and it puzzled Ben as to why she hadn't fallen in. He worked his boat to her location, pulled her into it and heard her astounding story: she was part of a party of five who had flown north from San Diego with the intention of canoeing the rivers. They got into serious trouble and she did not know the fate of the others.

Left with no other option, Ben started patrolling the other channels and came upon two men on a sandbar. He kept searching and found

Ben in the Grand Canyon of the Fraser River, 1974. Photo Ben Meisner.

another man, and shortly after that another woman was found. The entire party was rescued and could not express their gratitude enough. Ben got through by radio to the Alaska Coast Guard and they asked if he could take the party another 70 kilometres (42 miles) along the river to where a helicopter would meet them.

Well, the chopper was met and the party wanted to know what they owed Ben for the trip. The actual price would have floored them, as Ben had his fuel air-lifted in by helicopter at a cost of about $500 a barrel. He told them he only wanted a thank-you letter, which they promised would be forthcoming. Although that incident happened many years ago, the letter never arrived. Perhaps it is still moving around in the postal system. As to the real cost, Ben estimated it ran to about $1,500.

Just to get an idea of how much boating Ben has undertaken, he has been in rivers in all provinces except Quebec. His last two jet boats have accumulated over 5,000 hours. Ben pointed out that a great many jet boat accidents have taken place in the last few years. The number of them that have been smashed up, or completely destroyed, is stunning, to put it mildly. Just in the last few years, several boats have been lost in Fort George Canyon, along with two fatalities. Ben described how he was racing along with another jet boat and glanced over to see how the other guy was doing. A couple of seconds later he glanced over again and there was nothing there. The boat and operator were gone under the water. Nothing was ever found of man or boat.

Ben had a rather unusual story that some may find hard to believe, but my brother Clarence and I had already experienced the exact same thing. In this case, Ben and a doctor were hunting grizzlies along the railroad east of Prince George. It was in spring, when the grizzlies follow the railroad grade looking for train-killed moose. As the two men made their way along the grade, they spotted a grizzly. It was a good size, which usually means a smart bear. The bear spotted or scented them and disappeared into the heavy willows and brush along the grade. No luck, but the men went back again the next evening, and again the bear outsmarted them and made its escape.

At that point, the doctor suggested that the bear might have figured out that their arrival and departure was tied in with the noise of the boat they were using. Ben said he told the good doctor that he was nuts, in a nice sort of way. The doctor applied a bit of pressure and so, to make him happy, Ben agreed to give it a try. The doctor hid behind some brush as Ben walked back to his boat. He fired up the engine and drove just a short distance before he heard a rifle shot. The bear had indeed tied their coming and going to the noise of the boat motor.

When I asked Ben and his wife for their choice of the most scenic river, they agreed it had to be the Peace River. When asked which was the most dangerous, Ben chose the Fraser River. His favourite saying is "The Fraser River takes no prisoners."

⚓

I know many people who take great enjoyment jet boating the backcountry, but I honestly do not know any who enjoy it more than Kevin Fitzsimmons and Brent Gobbi of Prince George. These two men have experienced the extremes of jet boating. They have smashed boats, and they have gotten stuck in places where it takes much work and time to escape. They have raised the sport of jet boating to an unbelievable level. In fact, even after watching them perform I am left with the feeling that what I have just witnessed is impossible. They go through places where fish would have trouble navigating, and they jump over trees and logjams where only birds would dare. Because of this new-found ability, they manage to gain access to places of stunning beauty and grandeur.

In order to access some of these remote waterways, these boats are subjected to enormous loads, often carrying over 500 litres (110 gallons) of fuel, plus an abundance of gear. The heavier the load, the more damage the boats receive when they hit logs and rocks, or make jolting stops.

Brent got started in jet boating by purchasing an Ali-Craft, and it was not long before he and two buddies decided to run the Tuchodi River. In a place rightly referred to as "Boulder Alley," he put the new boat to a test. In one spot he bounced up onto some rocks. His helpful friends cut some trees to use as pry bars, and when he got the back of the boat into the water, one friend shouted to give it full power. Brent hit the power and the water being ejected out the back of the boat blew his helper clear into the icy water. Then Brent had to don a floater jacket and chest waders and cross the river with a line. In due course they winched the boat back to floating water. They knew there was a cabin somewhere up ahead so they made a run for it. The poor man in the wet clothing was at the point of surrendering to hypothermia by the time they reached the cabin and blessed warmth. It was Brent's first trip and he made his way to the insurance company office with a monster bill for damages.

Boulder Alley on the Tuchodi River. Photo Brent Gobbi.

Not a quitter, Brent had the boat repaired and it was back to the war games again. To make a long story short, he got into a spot where he plugged the jet with rocks and had to keep going. He ended up stuck tight. At that point two other boats came along, but they were in no position to help because they had problems of their own. They had gotten into a bind and came to a crashing stop. The results were one man with a terrible cut on his face, which meant they had to carry on and get medical attention. During his run through the rocks, Brent had torn a big hole in the rear of his boat, so water was pouring in and the bilge pump was running. He had some material with him designed to stop leaks, so he rammed it into place and headed for home. Under full power he got back to the launch site just as darkness was closing the day. When he returned to Prince George, it was back to the insurance company where the same agent greeted him with "You've got to be kidding!" Brent was not kidding; he had done another number on his Ali-Craft. He took the remains of his boat to a builder who looked at it and said, "Your boat is dead; it has taken its last gulp of water."

Some memories make him wince, such as the time he was zooming along Kenneth Creek only to meet another jet boat head-on, right in the bend of the stream. Once again there was a loud boom and some more dents. Another memory that makes Brent squirm concerns the time he was in a bad spot along a tributary of the Parsnip River and had to apply full power to get into deeper water. Unknown to him, the engine had blown a head gasket. By the time he realized what the problem was, it was too late. Another lesson learned and a bill for $2,500 for a new engine.

At this point Brent had used up all goodwill with the insurance company so he had to change plans. Good luck finally came his way when he met Kevin Fitzsimmons, owner of Omineca, a company that builds state-of-the-art jet boats in Prince George. Kevin's first words were "I'll build you a boat you can't wreck."

Well, the men went to work and about $70,000 later the boat was complete. A great deal of water has passed through the impellor of the new boat, and Brent recalls the time he beat the hell out of it in good old Boulder Alley, only to find that it had survived the beating without serious damage.

Brent does not mind admitting that he has learned a great deal from Kevin; they certainly have travelled some hazardous water together. Along the McGregor River is a stream called Jarvis Creek, which is a beautiful spot for boating. Some distance up the stream is a spot called The Rock, where all boats have had to retreat. But no one told Kevin and Brent that they had to stop there. With Kevin at the controls they managed to jump The Rock and were on their way into unexplored territory. The miles and logjams passed by and still they moved on. By following their progress on the map, I believe they came within a few miles of the Jarvis Lakes. Time and again they rounded a turn in the stream to find two or three divided creeks ahead, each with logs or boulders in the pathway. Often Kevin had to make split-second decisions, and he always

Brent's boat on the Muskwa River. Photo Brent Gobbi.

The many channels of the Tuchodi River. Photo Brent Gobbi.

seemed to take the right course. At one point I felt certain that I recognized a mountain peak and realized they were close to Mount Ida. This means that they must have gone at least 20 kilometres (12 miles) beyond The Rock. This is a fantastic achievement by any stretch of the imagination. I am aware of one particular spot they visited where humans have never trod, unless they landed in a helicopter.

Beaver dams present no obstacle to these boats and are not damaged by the intrusion. The bottoms of jet boats are covered with a sheeting of Kevlar, which allows them to slide over rocks and gravel bars without any damage. But the most obvious upside of these vessels is their ability to run streams at low-water levels, thereby eliminating the likelihood of damaging birds' nests along the banks. Outboard motors with propellers deep in the water often have no choice but to run small streams at higher water levels, thereby increasing the risk to birds' nests.

A builder of jet boats for several years, Kevin has raised the art of reading the water to a new level. Split-second decisions have to be made and made correctly; there is no allowance for error. It's called an extreme sport and rightly so, because they are walking right out on the edge most of the time. Brent adds a bit of humour to the sport of jet boating by saying, "You don't really need to have water anymore, but it helps."

~♨~

There is no question that jet boats have opened up the outback, allowing people into areas where boats have never gone, but the biggest change of all came along with the kayak. Suddenly daredevils are going over falls and through canyons where their forefathers perished. Thse new river rats simply roll over and continue on their thrilling way, where formerly these antics would have resulted in a certain death sentence.

Ian Norn of Prince George has been involved in kayaking and instructing for years, and he has remarkable photographic proof to support his claims. Has he had a few scares along the way? You bet he has. Among his souvenirs from the sport was a busted eardrum that took a month to repair itself. Ian has kayaked in such places as Whistler, Terrace and throughout central BC, as well as in California and New Zealand with his close friends Joe Kotai, Morgen Baldwin and Hardy Griesbauer. In total he has kayaked close to a hundred different rivers over the last 12 years, during which he has had many close calls. When I asked why he continues with kayaking he replied, "The camaraderie, spirit of adventure, and the adrenaline of paddling challenging rivers."

Ian Norn on Torpy Falls. Photo Ian Norn.

Joe Kotai, Upper Clore River. Photo Ian Norn.

I listened to many of Ian's hair-raising adventures and viewed the video of some canyon exploits. One trip he made was through Eight-Mile Canyon along the McGregor River. Only one short piece of canyon was portaged, where the river makes a 90-degree turn and rolls over on itself. If I hadn't seen it on video, I would not believe it possible.

Among Ian's adventures was the time he was paddling in Terrace on the upper Williams River, a stretch of class 4 water, when he realized he was off line. He tried to correct and in turn went over a pour-over sideways. Before he could roll back up, he hit his head against a rock, which delivered a hard blow to his ear. He saw stars, and when he did finally manage to roll up, all he could hear in his left ear was a loud static noise. It took about five minutes to regain his senses, only to make a poor decision: he would finish paddling the last 300 metres (1,000 feet). Upon paddling off a difficult 2-metre (6-foot) drop, he rolled up only to realize that he had lost all sense of balance. It was equivalent to being absolutely drunk and spinning around 20 times, then trying to walk straight. He struggled through even relatively easy water to get to shore. With the help of his friends he survived and was driven to the hospital where he learned he had perforated his eardrum. It was a month before he was back on the water.

Another incident ended with his hand getting jammed between his kayak and a rock. Result: a broken hand and having to decide whether it was easier to hike out of the deep canyon or paddle out the rest of the class 4–5 section of river. He chose to paddle out.

Joe Kotai is another active kayaker who started paddling in Prince George and then moved to Terrace. He is the epitome of the exploratory kayaker in that his greatest passion is finding new and unexplored rivers to challenge. During September 2009 Ian and Joe Kotai, along with two other kayakers, paddled a river flowing into the Douglas Channel. When they came to a small waterfall, Ian watched Joe run it safely and then chose to follow him. When he came down off the falls, he landed incorrectly and got pushed upside down into the more difficult right side of the stream. Several times he tried to roll up before he gave up and swam out of his kayak, a last-ditch response. He had travelled about 30 metres (100 feet) downstream before he managed to resurface in calmer water. With another class 5 rapid below, he had no choice but to cross the river to his friends on the opposite bank. They came to his rescue by tossing

Sean Fraser on the upper Cariboo River. Photo Ian Norn.

him a throw bag, which is a rope stuffed into a small bag designed to be thrown to a swimmer in trouble.

One week later, Ian, Joe, their friend Natou and two other friends flew in to Bernie Lake between Smithers and Terrace to paddle the Upper Clore River, a difficult class 5 canyon. On one of the most difficult rapids, Natou went first, had a close encounter with the left wall, but made it through. When Ian's turn came, he flipped and hit his head on rocks just under the surface. Having learned from his past incident, this time he was wearing a full-face helmet. Although Ian felt as if he had come close to breaking his neck, his helmet protected him and he was able to carry on. Later in the canyon, they came upon a difficult rapid that they chose to paddle after only one of them had looked it over. As they paddled into the rapid, one pour-over gave a couple of the kayakers trouble, causing one to swim the rest of the class 5 rapid, and another to receive a good thrashing for about 40 seconds before he luckily got bounced clear and paddled to safety. It was like riding a bucking bull and being in a washing machine at the same time. In the end, they paddled out of the canyon successfully, exhilarated and exhausted.

Chris Robberts has been one of the more active kayakers in the Prince George area for several years. Originally from South Africa, he has paddled such rivers as the Zambezi in Africa, as well as several in Nepal and throughout Canada.

Ian feels that he owes his life to Chris, who rescued him while paddling the Raft River near Clearwater, BC. Ian had rolled his kayak in a class 4 rapid, and upon righting himself found he was being pushed into a sieve, which is a jumble of rocks comparable to a spaghetti strainer. Ian managed to keep from being pushed completely underneath the rocks, and held himself until Chris came to his rescue and pulled him out. Had Chris not come to the rescue, Ian would have been pushed under the rocks, from which there was no escape as the exits were all smaller than his body. This is why a person should never kayak alone.

In the fall of 2005, Chris Robberts, Sean Fraser and Ian Norn decided to explore the upper McGregor River Canyon of central BC. All three men were aware that the history of this canyon is one of tragedy where several people and boats were lost. Their decision to go in the fall of the year was to avoid high water. Rumour has always had it that the canyon was impassable, so they took their time, carefully scouting the river along the way, cautious of what was around each bend. Along the way they paddled several class 4 rapids and encountered a class 5 rapid, which was also difficult to scout. Because they could not see far enough below the end of the rapid to ensure their safety, they decided to portage

Laura Bakerman on the upper Quesnel River.

Kim Ward Robberts on Dore River. Photo Ian Norn.

around. This portage required that they hike to the top of the canyon with their kayaks, only to decide they did not have enough time to continue down the river that day.

They hiked out 4 kilometres (2.5 miles) without their boats to the nearest road and returned two days later to venture back into the canyon and complete what they started. After lowering their boats, using ropes in places, they continued down the river through a series of difficult class 4 rapids until the canyon walls disappeared. In total, all the rapids along the canyon were kayaked except for one.

Among Ian's adventures was a kayaking trip through Hell's Gate in the Fraser Canyon. He found it very turbulent and unpredictable but managed through unscathed.

Ian has spent many summers exploring new rivers and kayaking familiar rivers in his backyard. Besides challenging himself, he enjoys introducing new people to the wonderful sport of kayaking in our magnificent wilderness.

I find it interesting to learn that Prince George and other communities throughout BC have several accomplished female kayakers, some having kayaked throughout the province, in other parts of Canada and even internationally. Morgen Baldwin, originally from Dome Creek, has kayaked as faraway as New Zealand on class 4-plus rivers. Laura Bakerman is known for running some wild water, and each year there are more women involved in the sport. Kim Ward Robberts has kayaked in such faraway countries as Nepal and South Africa. Both she and Laura reside in Terrace, which is a well-known kayaking paradise.

A century ago people no doubt stood at the top of canyons, rapids and whirlpools and knew that they would never be conquered. Since that time, not only kayakers but also whitewater rafters have proven them wrong. What does the future hold? Perhaps the next century will find people going places and doing things far beyond our present comprehension. What is impossible today may be routine tomorrow. One thing appears certain: every generation needs excitement and will go to any length to provide it. Something deep inside human beings seems to demand it.

Black bear eating buds up in a cottonwood tree. Photo courtesy Wes Westgarde.

Dog-tired after roaming the woods, Frank hit the sack and readily fell asleep. Along about the middle of the night he awoke to a crunching sound and switched on a light to behold the mama bear eating macaroni from his pack. He drove her away but she returned again and again. This continued until he was put in a position where he had to shoot her. The following day he left the area for four days and upon his return discovered the grizzly had found and eaten the mama bear with only its head left as evidence. Nearby he found a paw from one of the cubs. Surprisingly, after more than 50 years in the woods, this encounter was the only time he was bothered by bears.

Frank recalled another special memory involving a bear. He was driving near Mayo and passing through a grove of poplar forest when something high in a tree caught his eye. The trees were practically bare at the time because the buds were just coming out. This made the object stand out clearly. Frank drove just a short distance farther along before his curiosity got the better of him and forced him to turn around and go back for a second look. The dark object turned out to be a black bear that was perched high in the crotch of a tree that separated into three parts. As Frank and his partner watched, the bear repeatedly broke off branches and ran them through its mouth, eating all the available buds. The bear seemed at ease and looked intelligent. It was early spring so food was not readily available, but this bear managed quite well.

Frank and I got into a discussion about wolverines, and while he agreed with other trappers that they are extremely tough, he claimed he found them rather easy to trap. He described how he had nailed some moose meat to a tree and then placed traps and snares around the bait. When he returned to check the sets, he found that a wolverine with two large young had been there. The mama had got caught in a snare but had fought so hard that she had managed to break the wire. Two weeks later when he arrived at the set, he found the same wolverine in one of the traps. Upon examination, he could scarcely believe his eyes. The snare

9.

Bush Trails to Success

I have read that the chance of full-time prospectors hitting the big one is about one in two hundred, but this does not deter them one little bit. Just ask any of them and they have a million reasons for being out there in the rugged mountains, eating flies and mosquitoes, fighting alders and devil's club and all manner of buckbrush.

One such individual is a man named Frank Plut, who first felt the call of the woods when he was just a lad. Frank spent many winters falling timber for forest companies, which allowed him the freedom necessary to roam the woods in the summer months searching for minerals. After a few years of wandering the backcountry he took an interest in jade, an interest that turned into an obsession.

Frank also managed to purchase a trapline, so he spent many winters chasing furs through the woods. I asked him to relate some of his woods experiences, especially any problems he had encountered with bears. Echoing many other prospectors, he admitted that he had few problems with bears and suggested that if they see you, hear you or get your scent, they usually leave the area. One recollection took him back to an area north of Babine Lake that he had returned to after a short absence. Prior to his having left the area he had made two caches of food, one in a tree and the other on top of a huge boulder. On that same trip he had spotted a large grizzly digging on a mountain about a kilometre away. With a limited amount of food in his pack, he returned to the caches to find that a mother black bear with two cubs had found and devoured both caches He made camp and after hiking the woods all day, returned to spend the night.

Prospector Frank Plut.

had been set too wide, so the wolverine had managed to get the front half of her body through before she got caught. The snare had caught her behind the rib cage and was still around her body, which was compressed down to about 10 centimetres (4 inches). When he skinned it out, the hide fell apart. The animal was almost cut in half and yet it had travelled its line for two weeks. The strangest part of the story was that the other two wolverines had returned to the same site and both were caught. Frank's experiences with wolverines differed from those of many other trappers who found them exceedingly hard to trap. As for being tough, I know of nothing in nature that is tougher than a wolverine. A man who trapped the upper McGregor River area put it quite well when he stated, "If bears were as tough as wolverines for their size, I wouldn't go into the woods."

The summer of 1958 found Frank at Manson Creek, where he lived off the land, fishing, hunting and prospecting. At that time he met a former Barkerville prospector named Harold Bowey. The two men spent four years together and Frank learned a lot about the prospecting game. In time, Frank took out some gold placer claims on Ogden Mountain. He bought an old D8 Cat and worked the claims for a couple of years, then sold out. During that time he learned a great deal about jade. His next

move was to the Axel Gold Range, where he found some jade which he
flew out by helicopter. Because it was not a high grade of jade, the operation was a failure. Once again, Frank moved on.

In time, Frank moved his D8 Cat to the Yukon where he took up a
partnership with some people he had worked with years earlier. In total,
he spent three years around Whitehorse and then went back to Dease
Lake, where he worked for a different group of people hauling jade boulders out to Dease Lake. This was a 113-kilometre (69-mile) haul, which
required three days to get the boulders to Dease Lake and another two
days to make the return trip. He used to drill a hole through the boulders
and put a quick fix on the end, which had to be replaced several times
along the way. This was very slow and costly, so after three years he had to
give it up as a hopeless venture.

Finally, in 1980, Frank got his own jade property about 112 kilometres (70 miles) from Dease Lake. The following year his nephew Tony
Ritter came to Dease Lake and got involved with jade. He spent two
summers there and acquired valuable experience. Armed with a good
education, Tony went into jade mining in a big way. In fact, at present he
is one of the biggest jade producers in the world, which shows that there
is still room for success out there in the backcountry.

Frank signed his claims and camp over to Tony and then headed
for the Yukon again. This time he took gold claims near Mayo, where he
set up a camp and went to work with a hoe and D8 Cat. He's still there
and, with two helpers working with him, he hopes to buy another hoe
and take at least a couple hundred grand in the three months allowed by
nature at that latitude. However, as one prospector put it, "Giving out
information about gold is much like having your teeth pulled; it hurts so
you keep your mouth shut."

When I asked Frank to sum up his life he stated, "I did what I wanted
when I wanted; I always lived a life of freedom and that meant the most
to me." I wonder how many of us can say the same thing. But even more
important, to be able to live the life you prefer and come out with money
in the bank is equal to "having your cake and eating it too." Perhaps that
can be done.

I doubt that one can find a prospector who will not agree that there
is an excitement involved in prospecting that makes it a way of life that is
hard to give up. At the most, these people only do other tasks as a means

to find working money to carry on with their way of life. I honestly envy people who find their life's desire, and I certainly class Frank Plut in with that group. The intense interest that brightens his face when the subject is broached simply says it all.

Frank's nephew, Tony, is still working near Dease Lake, where he runs one of the biggest jade mines on the planet. He has several hoes, Cats and trucks and sells almost exclusively to the Chinese market. When I questioned Frank about the value of jade boulders, I was shocked when he told me about a sale that took place recently to Chinese buyers—two high-quality jade boulders, one weighing 17 tons and the other 24 tons, brought in a combined price of $2.3 million. Certainly that strikes me as almost talking about real money. Rumour has it that some of this jade is being used to build a 3-kilometre (2-mile) highway in China. I guess if you have it, you may as well flaunt it.

There is a timeless saying in the prospecting world that one should never work a claim that has been worked by Chinese miners. When one takes a look at how thorough they were, never leaving a stone unturned, it is easy to understand why that saying arose. Put another way, it is also acknowledged that Chinese prospectors can live well where the rest of us would starve to death.

Prospectors Frank Plut and David Humphreys.

I am aware of several people who have searched for gold along the Fraser River, including one of its tributaries, the Goat River, perhaps lured by tales of gold finds in the past. During the last few years I have put a lot of thought into this matter and here is what I believe happened. Readers may recall a story handed down by the Perry family of Prince George. This event took place in 1912 when an aged prospector came down the Fraser River on a raft. Suffering from scurvy and starvation, he was taken to the Grand Trunk Pacific Railway Hospital at Willow River. In short order it was discovered that he had two quart jars full of gold nuggets. When questioned as to the whereabouts of his gold find, he kept his silence and the secret went to the grave with him. Now let's pursue this story because it gets more interesting.

During the 1930s four Chinese prospectors arrived in Prince George with a respectable amount of gold and openly admitted they had found it along the Goat River. To the best of my knowledge no decent amount of gold has been found upriver of Prince George since that time. This begs an explanation. Let's assume that the old prospector found his gold along the Goat River, and then let's assume that he believed

Goldfinder. Photo Brian Marynovich.

he got all of it. Would it not follow that he would have no reason to keep it secret? Now let's assume that the four Chinese prospectors came along about 20 years later and found the same strike. When they arrived in Prince George they openly announced the location of their strike. Does it not make sense that they spoke out only because they believed

Chinese miners turned every stone at the Christie lead near McDame Creek. Photo David Humphreys.

they got all the gold? And I'm going to suggest that if these Chinese miners figured they got all of the gold remaining in that strike, then that was exactly the case.

Now I'm going to stick my neck out and state that I believe this is exactly what happened: the Chinese miners cleaned up all that remained of the old man's original strike and therefore had no intention of returning to the Goat River. Since it appears that no exciting amount of gold has been found along the Goat River since that time, what other possibilities are there? If anyone has an alternative theory, I'm more than willing to listen.

Sometimes people involved in the prospecting business find far more than they bargain for. Such was the case recently in the Yukon, when word was flashed to the outside world of an astounding find. Just a few days later I opened an email from my nephew Dave Humphreys, an avid prospector, and to my surprise I found a picture of this amazing fossil. As it turned out, the picture had been taken by a long-time friend of Dave's named David Mack, who found the fossil while running an excavator at 60-Mile River in the Yukon. These two men had spent years prospecting in the Yukon, and because of their friendship I was able to receive the following email from David Mack:

On June 9th, 2010 I was working the excavator on night shift and dayshift so the days get all mixed up. After we had stripped off 40 feet of mud with the dozers, I came along with the excavator to dig a drainage ditch so the pay gravel would thaw quicker. Well on that night I was digging away but it got rather dark so I put my headlights on. I had my iPod going and was just digging along when I came out with a bucket of dirt. The teeth in the bucket had caught one of the tusks and pulled it upwards. Then it rolled and stood on the back of the skull with the head sideways to me and the tusks still attached. I sort of spotted it out of the corner of my eye, with the lights not directly on it, so I couldn't quite figure out what it was. As it was kind of sideways to me the first thought that entered my mind was, "My God! I woke up the devil." Then when I managed to shine my lights on it and got a closer look, I almost went in my pants. I got off the machine and wiped some of the dirt off it and then I felt a strange realization that I was the first person to see and touch this strange creature. Finally, I brought it to camp, cleaned it off and then pictures were taken, but none of me.

As stated, David Mack was working a backhoe for a mining company at 60-Mile River when he pulled up something worth more than its

weight in gold. A woolly mammoth, estimated to be about 30,000 years old, and with the skull intact. It didn't take long for the Yukon's only paleontologist, Grant Zazula, to arrive at the scene, and it took even less time for word to reach the outside world.

Dave Humphreys and David Mack at 60-Mile River, 2008.
Photo David Humphreys.

The skull, which is about 1.5 metres long and 2 metres high (5 feet by 6.6 feet), weighed 115 kilograms (250 pounds), and was found under 30,000-year-old volcanic ash. A few ribs and a shoulder blade were also recovered. After a perusal of the find Zazula stated, "We see bones all the time, but I've never seen a whole skull intact; I don't think a find like this has been found for 100 years. The only recorded evidence of a mammoth skull found in the Yukon is an archival photograph of three miners sitting beside one in 1901. That skull was featured in the Chicago World's Fair, but was soon lost or destroyed," he added. Researchers are getting closer to cloning a mammoth, according to Zazula. "It's not a matter of if, but a matter of when."

David Mack deserves credit for unearthing this fossil, yet as is so often the case, he has received none whatsoever. The *Yukon News* displayed a picture of the paleontologist posing with the skull, but not one of Mack. I understand that the newspapers have to go with what they get, but is it not strange how the glory always seems to go to those who least deserve it? I notice that the fossil has been named Flynn, in honour of the mine manager who donated it. I suppose that is fair, but no mention or picture of David Mack? Without his sharp eye to recognize that it was a treasure, there might have been little more than a few bone fragments hanging in some museum.

Mammoth skull. Photo David Mack.

There are times when a person lucks out and gets great pictures without working for them. An example occurred recently when Mike Boyle was on his way to work along the Alaska Highway. A vehicle had struck and killed a deer and just as the men were passing, two adult grizzlies wandered out of the woods and went straight to the carcass. With utter contempt for the vehicles and people watching, they went to work devouring the animal. One picture shows a grizzly with blood on its snout staring at the intruders as if to say, "If you want it, come and try to get it!"

When the bears had taken their fill, they held a love fest and didn't appear to give a hoot if people were watching or not.

So what does the future hold for people going into the woods? I think the outlook is bleak because I agree with the woodsmen who say that both grizzlies and black bears are losing their fear of humans. Or perhaps it is more accurate to state that most bears have already lost their fear of humans. This spells trouble for people going into the woods. The two men who were mauled recently in their tent south of Nelson got a double surprise. They were mauled at night, and when they returned the following day they found where the grizzly bear had cut their trail and then followed their tracks until it found them at their tent. If this is true, it raises the bar a few more notches.

Every year it appears to be getting worse. Now it is common for bears to refuse to move when encountered. Even lowly black bears are becoming more aggressive. Gunshots in the woods are equivalent to ringing dinner bells for grizzly bears. I know people who are reluctant to hunt in the evenings, because if they do not have time to remove the animals from the woods, by the time they return the next morning the grizzlies have claimed the kills.

Grizzly: "If you want it, come and get it."
Photo Mike Boyle.

I'm going to stick my neck out and state that I believe we have reached the point where we have far too many bears in parts of BC. I hope to be proven wrong when I predict that more and more people will be mauled every year unless drastic action is taken or a better defence mechanism is found. Finding a new defence against bears is an absolute must, since bears have become the major obstacle confronting people going into the woods. Surely it is incumbent upon government to put some effort into this field because many of the people at risk are government employees. Personally, I put very little faith in pepper sprays. I carried them for a short while when I was with the Ministry of Forests, but thankfully I never had to use them. Others have assured me that the sprays are vastly overrated. Let us not forget about the two women who used an entire can of bear spray against a mother grizzly with cubs in Glacier Park. The bear paid no attention whatsoever and severely mauled both women.

It seems strange that we have weapons such as tasers to use on people, but nothing effective to use against bears except firearms, which are so final and difficult to carry.

I firmly believe that wild animals must remain wild with a fear of humans; anything less will mean increasing aggressiveness with the resulting bear attacks on humans. If others disagree with me, let them put it in writing. The future will determine which is right, and I will not mind at all if I am proven wrong.

Some prospectors who have spent decades in the woods without having problems with bears now admit that they are worried about them. People in general tell me that there appear to be black bears everywhere and quite often the bears have no fear whatsoever.

A fortune has been spent trying to deal with problem bears. For years the bears were trapped and hauled by truck or flown to remote areas, hoping they would adapt and stay there. Instead they return home time and again, each time having lost more weight, until they perish. In the past I have repeatedly misjudged bear behaviour because I underestimated their intelligence; this time I don't intend to do that. I believe that bears experience many of the same feelings and emotions as humans. When we are taken from our homes we feel a powerful homesickness. There is an overwhelming urge to return. Could bears experience the same sort of thing? Why do they refrain from eating and exert all their energy into getting back to where they came from? Perhaps this is the reason why relocating bears has been such a dismal failure.

And so, what is the proper course in dealing with problem bears? Are we approaching a time when bears will openly hunt humans? Animal rights activists are walking on thin ice when they want to stop all hunting of bears. I think that while they might mean well, they are using the worst possible approach. Why is it almost impossible to get people to admit

that sometimes there are far too many bears for the animals' food supply? In part because of the mild winters with fewer den deaths, there appear to be more cubs per litter than in the past. Along with limited hunting, this has led to an astounding increase in bear populations. We can remove every edible thing — in fact we can even sterilize our communities in an effort to keep bears away — but it is destined to fail. In late fall, after the berry crops are gone, bears wander around aimlessly in search of food. This is easy to prove: if bears are travelling in a fairly straight line, their noses are leading them to food. But if they are just wandering around then they will go anywhere, including the streets of towns. There is only one solution: control population numbers.

Surely no sensible person can deny that the increase in bear numbers and the increase in their aggressive behaviour go hand in hand. I am absolutely certain that the increase in grizzly bear numbers explains the reason I found so many grizzlies chasing other grizzlies during the last five years that I studied them and shot videos. Yet not once did I find this during the first 40 years or so that I spent both hunting and studying bears in the same area. This means that the increase in grizzlies over the years has led to a dramatic change in their behaviour. They have become far more aggressive in their dealings with other grizzlies and humans.

Several years ago we were faced with a similar problem. There were too many black bears, but many people lived in the outback at that time and we just used common sense to control the numbers. When the bears got too numerous and started hanging around the communities, they were thinned out. Believe me, when bears find the carcass of another bear with human scent around it, they get the message loud and clear. Without a doubt they are smart enough to understand and they become wild animals again.

In short, the solution to the problem is simple: rather than close the season on bears, open it and watch the aggressive behaviour drop in direct proportion to the number of animals taken. This is not a guess; this is exactly what has taken place in the past. When we hunted bears a great deal it was almost impossible to get close to them. They ran away at the slightest indication of danger. In other words, we forced them to become wild animals once again.

I have had success in getting a mother grizzly with cubs or yearlings to move away by coughing at them, the same sound they make. This has been captured on video. I decided to try this method after I saw families of grizzlies move on when coughed at by other bears. What is most notable is that the bears did not get excited; rather they just walked away. It seems obvious that they would be foolish to attack another bear, which may turn out to be a large boar that could cripple or kill them.

However, the way I remember it, in the cases where I coughed I had the wind in my favour, so I don't know how mothers will respond if they have already detected human scent when the confrontation takes place. In that event perhaps coughing will have no deterrent value at all. As well, one must make certain not to cough at a lone or male bear, as they may take it as a challenge and act accordingly. It is my wish that wildlife officials make a conscious effort, when the situation allows, to determine if coughing is an effective defence against families of bears, both blacks and grizzlies.

Recently John Broderick got a surprise while at his farm in Dome Creek about 130 kilometres (80 miles) east of Prince George. He had just got out of bed when he heard something bawling in the distance, which he assumed was a cow moose. He drank a cup of coffee and then went outside again to check if the animal was still bawling. It was, so he asked his son-in-law to accompany him in trying to find the troubled moose. They jumped on their quads and headed in the direction of the noise, occasionally stopping to get their bearings. At last they came upon a moose calf lying dead beside an old road. The signs showed that a bear had dragged it a short distance to get it out of some water where it had dropped. The two men went just a little farther and found the mother moose in a field. She let out another mournful call and then left the area, having finally given up on her baby. This is a rather common occurrence during the months of May, June and July, when calf moose are easy targets for bears and wolves. Cow moose generally keep their calves close to water as a means of escape, because they can out-swim bears with ease.

I wish people would drop the love affair with predators. Perhaps it is time someone took up the cause of cow moose as they desperately try to raise their calves against so many enemies. I know from experience that black bears are a constant threat to these calves. The mother will fight to defend her young, but bears only need a couple of seconds, when the mother moose is occupied, to rush in and cripple the calf. Then they can just bide their time until the mother has to leave to get water or food. It is the same with wolves. One wolf will distract the mother by getting her to chase it, while another rushes in to attack the calf. When people see dry cow moose, they are prone to saying there is a shortage of bull moose, when in fact she may have had young and lost them to predators.

We are not alone with our bear problems. In parts of Russia, huge brown bears have reached unprecedented numbers and in a few cases have been found travelling in packs. The Kamchatka Peninsula is suspected of having the densest grizzly, or brown bear, population on the planet, estimated at 12,000 to 15,000. Recently elders from the villages of Khalino and Korf pleaded with authorities to send hunters to thin out the 30 bears that had surrounded their towns and forced the people to cower in fear. The list of people mauled and killed goes on and on.

If it is true that people mauled by bears often do not make the news, then they are indeed in a sorry state. A photographer named Michio Hoshino openly camped out near brown bears and was killed by them. His screams echoed through the night as the bear tore him to pieces, but because of a ban on firearms his unarmed friends camping in a nearby building were unable to assist him. I guess these bears never read the same book and didn't know they were supposed to be harmless.

On Sakhalin Island in Russia, three women were killed recently by grizzlies, and another woman was killed in the city where she lived. Some authorities have assumed that the problem is caused by a shortage of salmon. Whatever the cause, the result is perfectly obvious: there are too many bears for the available food supply.

An event that shook up the entire country occurred last year when geologists working for a mine refused to leave their quarters after two guards were killed by bears. Information from the mine stated that up to 30 huge bears had the place surrounded, and mine management pleaded for hunters to be sent to thin out the grizzlies.

I notice that some people blame a lack of experience around bears for the deaths, but if that were true why is it that the best-known grizzly expert in Russia, Vitaly Nikolayenko, was killed and eaten by a grizzly he had followed? With 25 years of experience around these bears, if he did not know them, what pseudo-expert possibly could? As was the case with Timothy Treadwell and his girlfriend, who were killed and eaten by a grizzly in Alaska, Vitaly was hanging around this bear just before den time, when food is least available. The song lyrics "When will they ever learn?" come to mind.

I found it most interesting that Vitaly had an empty can of pepper spray beside his half-eaten body. Once again we have proof that pepper sprays are an ineffective deterrent. Another downside to pepper sprays is that if the bear attacks us downwind, the spray will come right back in our own faces. Let's hope that the bears don't get addicted to pepper sprays.

What may be the sorriest part of this debacle is that the decisions on how to deal with problem bears in Russia are made by people who reside in the cities. That may be the reason why the cries for help in the tiny bush towns have been, in their inhabitants' own words, frequently ignored. It seems terribly wrong that people living in cities can decide that people working in remote areas cannot defend themselves against these marauding monsters.

I notice that there has been a lot of conflict going on in the Kam-chatka area of Russia. While some people have pleaded with the authorities to control bear populations, others have done everything in their power to protect the brown bears, even to the point of feeding and taming the bear cubs and yearlings. This turned out to be a no-brainer; the tamed bears were easy targets for the hunters and trappers, many of whom are licensed to harvest the bear hides for sale on the fur markets.

Time and again the message put out by wildlife personnel falls on deaf ears—a habituated bear is a dead bear.

So let's keep an eye on how they deal with their bear problems in the Kamchatka Peninsula. Perhaps we can learn from their errors or, more hopefully, their successes.

10.

HUMOUR AND OTHER POEMS

On August 9, 2005, my niece Alannah Wheeler left this world at too young an age. After many years of service to others in hospitals and therapy wards, it is my wish that she has gone to a better place. Alannah took an intense interest in poetry and, in my humble opinion, became rather adept at it. It is my hope that people will relate to and enjoy the following, which is my favourite of all her poems.

THAT NASTY OLD ROOSTER OF MINE

That rooster of mine, he's five years old, and never you've seen a rooster so bold.
Meanest rooster around I'm told; that nasty old rooster of mine.

Gathering eggs is a terrible fate; that rooster, Bart, is so full of hate.
He'll soon have you runnin' for the chicken coop gate; that nasty old rooster
of mine.

He guards his flock with his very life; with a beak that's as sharp as a butcher knife.
Even a weasel will run for its life from that nasty old rooster of mine.

Ever awake, ever aloof, my own scarred head is the living proof.
His favourite perch is the chicken coop roof; that nasty old rooster of mine.

Not an ounce of fear is in his heart; no matter how big, he'll tear you apart.
Anything that moves is a target for Bart; that nasty old rooster of mine.

No longer the king of the chicken coop; no longer the guard of his faithful group.
For today old Bart's in my chicken soup; that nasty old rooster of mine.

I have always loved a good poem, especially with a twist of humour. From the time I was a youngster Robert Service always touched me. For many years I had almost all his poems committed to memory. But time moves on, and since then I have switched to a poet with a profound sense of humour—Brian Salmond of Fort St. John. Brian has the ability to put words together in a humorous manner that makes me drool. I sincerely thank him for the use of his poems, four of which follow.

WORMIN' THE BARNCATS

Those cats have always been there or so it seems to me
They cruised the place in strict patrol and kept it vermin free
Though Spotty was the point man and always fought the strays
While Pete and Bill would cheer him on in snide but catty ways

His ears were always tattered like the attitude he packed
He was destined as a kitten, it's the way his deck was stacked
He would stand his ground and show the world his barn-race feline rap

He kind of had it in for me for surgery at home
That neutralized his rambling ways and doused the urge to roam
We hoped he'd never hold a grudge to implications of the deed
So we fed him good and kept him warm and met his every need

We're off to do some barnyard chores; then worm those stinking cats
Now there's potions and there's lotions and some capsules in the pills
It seems to me we've tried them all and they're fine by Pete and Bill

But Spotty takes exception to the basics of the rule
Since he's been had it's awful hard to take him for a fool
We think we have his number now; this stuff's in liquid form
And maybe he'd believe it's milk if we fed it to him warm

It'll be so fast he won't have time to either blink or cringe
We can tell he's not agreeing; there's a twitching in his eye
With dilated pupils and a smirk that's kind of shy

His razor claws extended and his hair all stood on end
He was puffed and poised for scrapping; he'd never break or bend
With leather gloves and waders that are duct-taped where they stop
And an insulated snowsuit to protect me at the top

I'll throw a nelson on him and most likely win the round
But he unloads his fury on me like a buzz saw gone berserk
The strangle hold that I've applied just isn't going to work
He's shredding up my clothing and the stuffing starts to fly
A slashing and a gashing like some rabid Samurai

His jaws were pried wide open with completion in our sight
When the kid was getting nervous and his aim was kind of bent
He hit the trigger way too quick and in my mouth it went

My eyes went crossed and I wheezed a lot as my blood began to boil
But lately I've been feeling great and sleeping through the nights
My stride is full of spring and I'm free of parasites.

REAL WEST CHICKEN OMELETTE

Take one good-sized hunting territory with camps that need supplies
Blend in a cheap but thrifty boss with dollars in his eyes
Fold in a bunch of youngsters and a Native guide or two
Now sprinkle in a camp cook and some hunters' first debuts

"The eggs, we forgot to pack some eggs, and they seem in short supply."
"So run you kids, go search the stacks, the barn, and the shed across the
    road.
Then you can be my hero 'cause you found the mother lode."

Then there they are; 21 large grade A cackleberries fresh from the farm.
They ain't posted with expiry dates so what the heck's the harm?
So with the heart of Morgentaler you beat the hen right off the nest
Then cart off all the eggs you can and come back for the rest

Then somewhat slyly you scrub them up in store-bought blocks of 12's
Well, who can tell the difference now? They're just like on the shelves.
So you pack them up for the morning trail—they ain't exploded yet.
So they make the 10-hour packathon and now the stage is set.

The dawn comes cracking early with the glimmer to the east.
The cook stove is a popping while the camp cook plans a feast.
Coffee strong with flapjack, and bacon on the side
And a huge old western omelette, her best in special pride.

We're down yonder saddlin' horses, finding out the way
When we hear the scream of terror in a most peculiar way.
And there goes cookie leavin' town, her hand across her mouth
She's out behind the woodpile and she's heavin' north and south.

We raced into the cookhouse, to see what made her sick
And there he lay, a sibling, that little unborn chick.
His buggy eyes are closed up tight, his little wings are crossed
Like a prehistoric reptile from an era long since lost.

And he's not smellin' awful good according to my nose.
I don't think he can stand the heat as far as chicken goes.
And then the question tripped my mind and hung there like a plague.
Which one hit the pan first, the chicken or the egg?

So I took it as my duty to remove him from the scene
My southern pride don't look so hot in paling shades of green
I wheel to leave and meet the hunters wide-eyed at the door
"You boys look extra hungry, should I cook a couple more?"

Brian Salmond and singer/songwriter Tom Cole live in Fort St. John. Fortunately they have teamed up to form an impressive combo. They have put out several CDs that I find priceless. In fact, I spend many evenings listening to their touching poems and songs. You can find them at www.tomcole.net.

This is another poem of Brian's that expresses his boundless sense of humour, and it is appropriately titled.

COST OF BEING FREE

The swap show crashed the air waves with some lady's high-pitched voice
She had these pups to give away to a good home of her choice.
My wife was listening to the program and scratched the number down.
Her mother was border collie; her sire tramped the better part of town.

It was thus on Easter morning that Jo pledged the pup to me
A real kind gift to call my own; the kind that's given free.
The term free became redundant as we met this friendly pup
It cost us fifteen bucks for gas to go and pick her up.

And we swung down past the feed store for a bag of puppy grow.
We wound up buying seven 'cause the sale was on you know.
A collar and a training leash and a ball for her to fetch
Some pigs' ears and a rawhide chew to help her down the stretch.

And tomorrow we must phone the vet to take her for her shots
They're 80 bucks and she needs three so they'll be costing lots.
Then Jo booked her in obedience school to keep us both in line.
And tho' they claimed that I was slow the dog was learnin' fine.

But I was welcome to pay the bills with cash or credit card.
I never relished either one 'cause I thought they hit me hard.
I'm clinching bad and cringing; there's a ringing in my ear
The cash machine's a singing tunes I really dread to hear.

But the pup is really growing; she's sailing for the top
'Til I took her to the field with me to help me cut some crop.
She got tangled in the binder knife and cut up all her legs
I got a nightmare vision of my good cow dog on pegs.

But my vet friend works his magic and eases all my woes
He sews her up and sews them on and sews on all her toes.
And then he hands the bill to me; I'm hanging on the fence.
My eyes bulge out at fifteen big ones and thirty-seven cents.

But I'm hell forever grateful that my dog can run and play.
I cringe and shudder in disbelief and sign the cheque to pay.
And soon she's runnin' on all fours; she's healed up really good.
We decide to take her with us to go cut a load of wood.

Now this part of my story tends to injure me a little.
We load the dually high with wood; then drive across her middle.
But she survived it and this could make you freak
She was loping slow across the yard within a given week.

So life rolls on and now it's time to have the pot hound spayed.
In tribute to a better way of lifestyle that's been laid.
But soon the phone is ringing; Dr. Dick is in dismay
He claims he's never seen a pooch so muddled up this way.

She's been run on through a blender and then dried out in the sun.
And square-baled just to top it off; I think your dog is done.
Don't quit us now, Doc, the money is not an issue
I sniffed my nose and dabbed my eyes with a square of toilet tissue.

So he stripped her ubilus, stretched her pedigal and cranked her
    rudder straight.
Then sewed her up and gave her life and she's here to demonstrate.
And the bill's a couple cool ones, but that don't matter none
She's safe at home within a week; another battle won.

But in the greater picture; it's obvious to me
We couldn't afford to keep her if we hadn't got her free.

I do not know how one person can crank out so many good poems. Perhaps Brian has a whole herd of writers locked up in his hay barn. Anyway, here is another poem of his that I absolutely adore.

THE SHEEP DOG

They said Wesley's ranch was rustic if it wasn't for the sheep,
and he never would have kept them if they hadn't helped him sleep.
For each night on his pillow he would count them two by two,
And for every night he rested well he thanked each ram or ewe.
He was busy calving heifers with a heavy run on twins,
With most the size of yearlings; his nerve was running thin
But when the old ewe took to lambing, he simply wasn't there;
'til he found her in the morning with her four feet in the air.
But Mary had birthed her little lamb and he was still alive,
And was searching for his breakfast from the moment he'd arrived.
As Wesley pondered at his fate, he knew just how to rig it;
His old cow dog had just had pups and possessed an extra spigot.
And she seemed to understand his plight as she gazed upon her spawn;
She knew he had a need for life and finally took him on.
He started thinking dog-like as he took his turn to nurse;
He'd simply learn the canine ways; a sheep could sure do worse.
He took his turn in puppy play and was quick to fetch a stick;
He'd sit and roll, and right off hand, they taught him not to lick.
He grew up fast and proper, and seldom chased a cat;
Or howled at night, or tramped around, he knew where home was at.
He trimmed the shrubs and lawn grass and kept it fertilized;
And there was no messy dog scats, 'cause his was sanitized.
He'd bring the milk cows down the lane and hold them at the gate
He'd have them there at 6 o'clock and never once was late.
And as far as not producing, you could shear him twice a year,
His hybrid poop smelled profit, as the evidence was clear.
The legend spread throughout the land on the habits of the creature,
And reporters drove for days and nights to scoop this special feature.

Psychologists and media converged upon his place
And Wesley welcomed one and all, a smile upon his face.
There's a code that rules the ways out West that never should be lost
A legacy of Western folk; upheld at any cost.
Old Wesley loved his sheep dog and fondly named him Rover.
He flipped a coin that fateful day and had to think it over.
You're a little late my friend and it hurts just like the Dickens;
We put him down just yesterday, we caught him killing chickens.
And if you think we miss him, you're right on top the button
But pull up a stump and grab a plate, the wife is serving mutton.

STRANGE SAYINGS

Wanderers of the woods and mountains often have spare time in which to think up odd sayings. How about the guy who was forever holding others hostage with his endless chatter? He was put in his place when an observer said, "You must have brushed your teeth with gunpowder this morning because you can't stop shooting off at the mouth."

And then there was the young lad fresh from university who was humbling his friends with his boundless knowledge. Finally unable to bear his arrogance, one of his former friends said, "Before you get too carried away, try to remember that the Ark was built by amateurs while the *Titanic* was built by professionals."

This story held a special significance for me, because it brought back the following memory. Back in the 1950s I was offered a job cutting trail for BC Forest Service. The young lad who was selected to work with me had just returned from university, and much like the gentleman in the previous story knew pretty well everything worth knowing in the entire universe. Toward evening of the first day, we arrived at our starting point and made camp for the night. The next morning we ate breakfast and I immediately set about making a large lunch as we wouldn't be back in camp until late evening. I noticed that my partner was not doing likewise so I suggested he do so. His reply was short and sweet: "I don't need a lunch, I just ate and I'm not hungry."

We struggled along the old trail, cutting downed trees and brush as we went, so by the time noon rolled around I was thoroughly famished. I sat there eating my lunch while the bundle of wisdom sat watching me and drooling at the mouth, but too proud to do a little begging and admit he had been wrong. Out of mercy, I pulled out three large sandwiches I had brought along in anticipation of his change of heart. Believe it or not, he ate more than I did. During the rest of that trip, any time he got carried away with his own importance I would say, "I'm not hungry. I just ate!" It took quite a few years for him to live that down.

There is always room for humour out there in the woods, and rightfully some of this humour lives on for many years. Earl Dingwall of Prince George told me one of the best keepers I have ever heard. Back in 1958 Earl worked for Jim Chambers who owned a sawmill near Dome Creek, about 120 kilometres (75 miles) east of Prince George. During that summer two young men arrived in camp to take over as cook and flunky. Well it didn't take long to realize that these lads couldn't "parboil shit for a tramp," as the old saying went. The crew pleaded with Jim to fire them but he was too soft-hearted. Instead, Jim advised the crew that they had to find a way of getting the lads to quit.

A lot of thought went into their planning before they came up with a beauty of a trick. Jim had taken a fine boar grizzly back in the mountains a short time earlier and this was to be their weapon of choice. Just as the two lads were finishing up with the dishes and cleaning the cookhouse for the evening, three men went to work. Along with his twin brother Beryl, and close friend Maurice Schultz, Earl pulled the huge bear hide over his head and went to the window right near where the two lads were working. With an abundance of roars and a lot of slaps to the window frame and wall, Earl watched the lads go into panic mode. They put some boxes on top of the barrel stove and together they made it into the attic, all the while screaming that they were going to die. For the best part of an hour Earl did his bit by banging the walls and roaring. Then Maurice climbed up on the roof of the adjacent shed and continued to growl and pound on things.

The results were evident the next morning when the crew came into the cookhouse for breakfast. The two men were standing with their luggage packed, waiting for the passenger train to arrive in the community. During the rest of their wait, they regaled the crew with their horror stories of the previous night. When they described the size of the grizzly bear that had attempted to kill them, there could be no doubt—this bear was definitely a new world's record. That story has lived on through the years and probably has many more years to go.

�⸺⟣

If there has ever been a subject that has been discussed more then the weather, I certainly have not known about it. With that in mind, I think it is appropriate to tell the following story, which took place in Kamloops about 40 years ago. A group of forestry students was attending a rather advanced course in weather study to assist them in understanding fire behaviour. Among the students was a man named Ron Mould who was stationed in Kitimat at the time. It seems he was not entirely agreeing with everything the instructors said, so one of them asked, "Say, Ron, do you have a problem with weather forecasting?"

Back came the response: "I sure do, and you would too if you knew how many times I have shovelled two feet of partly cloudy."

�⸺⟣

Sometimes an event can be both troublesome and humorous at the same time. During the summer of 1981 I was employed by the Ministry of Forests. One morning I was travelling east on Highway 16 from Prince George when my fun day started. An approaching pickup truck began flashing its lights on and off, while at the same time the driver applied his brakes and pulled to the edge of the highway. As soon as I stopped, he rushed to my truck and shouted, "You better do something because the bridge is washing out a few miles from here."

People who are familiar with the Bowron Bridge, about 60 kilometres (35 miles) east of Prince George, will understand why I responded with "That's impossible. How could it wash out? Did the river come up real high?"

"No, there's a big creek washing it out."

Naturally I replied, "There is no creek running in there. You must be mistaken."

The fellow was quite clearly upset, but in all honesty I didn't believe him. Since I was going in that direction anyway I had no choice but to check it out for myself. About 10 minutes later I drove across the bridge to behold an unbelievable sight. A large stream was pouring down the east bank of the river and had already broken up and washed away the apron supporting the east approach to the bridge. At once I realized that disaster was imminent unless immediate action was taken, as pieces of cement were starting to fall out of the main roadway where the traffic was moving atop the bridge. Traffic had to be stopped and soon.

As I grabbed my radio to alert district office, I fully realized that this was going to be fun because they were not going to believe me. I got them on the radio and told them that the police and the Department of Highways had to be notified because the Bowron Bridge was washing out. Silence followed and then someone asked, "How can it be washing out?"

I could hardly refrain from laughing as I answered, "That big stream on the east side of the bridge is washing it out."

This time there was a prolonged silence and it was obvious that some heavy-duty discussions were going on back at the office. And then a gruffer, sterner voice came on. "I was out there yesterday, Jack, and there is no stream on the east side of the Bowron Bridge."

I was really enjoying it by this time, and I said, "There is now."

"Where did it come from?"

"I have no idea, but it is there, and it is a big stream."

It took a bit more time, but I finally convinced them to take action. Then I got some passersby to assist me so we could flag down the traffic and prevent a tragedy. Half an hour later a helicopter arrived and managed to solve the mystery. About 7 centimetres (3 inches) of rain had fallen the night before and the accumulating water was more than some huge beaver dams could hold. The dams were right on the height of land and they had previously been funnelling water in a southerly direction, but when they washed out they forged a new channel in a westerly direction. This caused a massive amount of water to create a stream where none had been before.

When I finally arrived back at the office late that same day, one of my co-workers told me that for a short period of time they figured I had flipped my lid. I assured him that I had experienced the exact same feeling when I first learned of it.

Acknowledgements

I offer a special thanks to the following people for their assistance in this endeavour. First off, I must thank the *Prince George Citizen* and the *Valley Sentinel* and other newspapers for referring to articles from the distant past. As well, I thank Betty Frank, Maxine and Peter Koppe, Pam and Geoff MacDonald, Ian Norn, Leon Lorenz, Vern Goglin, Frank Plut, David Mack, Steve and Rod Marynovich and David Humphreys for sharing their adventures with me.

Finally, I offer a special thanks to Steve Buba and Eric Klaubauf for their assistance and endless patience.

MORE GREAT READS BY CAITLIN PRESS

Trappers and Trailblazers, Jack Boudreau
Adventure/Local History ISBN 978-1-894759-39-7, 6 x 9, 256 pp, pb, b&w
photos, $22.95

Sternwheelers and Canyon Cats, Jack Boudreau
Adventure/Local History ISBN 978-1-894759-20-5, 6 x 9, 256 pp, pb, b&w
photos, $18.95

Wild & Free, Frank Cooke, as told by Jack Boudreau
Local History ISBN 1-894759-04-4, 6 x 9, 272 pp, pb, b&w photos, $24.95

Double or Nothing: The Flying Dur Buyer of Anahim Lake, Darcy Christensen
Memoir/Local History ISBN 978-1-894759-47-2, 6 x 9, 224 pp, pb, b&w
photos, $24.95

Jacob's Prayer, Lorne Dufour
Local History/Memoir ISBN 978-1-894759-33-5, 5.5 x 8, 160 pp, pb, b&w
photos, $18.95

North of Iskut: Grizzlies, Bannock and Adventure, Tor Forsberg
Local History/Memoir ISBN 978-1-894759-42-7, 6 x 9, 216 pp, pb, b&w
photos, $24.95

Edge of the Sound: Memoirs of a West Coast Log Salvager, Jo Hammond
Local History/Memoir ISBN 978-1-894759-49-6, 6 x 9, 256 pp, pb, b&w
photos, $24.95

Surveying Northern British Columbia: A Photo Journal of Frank Swannell,
Jay Sherwood
Local History/Biography ISBN 1-894759-05-2, 10.5 x 10.5, 166 pp, pb, b&w
photos, $29.95

The Railroader's Wife: Letters from the Grand Trunk Pacific Railway,
Jane Stevenson
Local History/Railroad ISBN 978 1-894759-43-4, 6 x 7, 196 pp, pb, b&w
photos, $24.95